In the Name of Mozart

© 2006 by Leuven University Press / Universitaire Pers Leuven / Presses Universitaires de Louvain, Blijde-Inkomststraat 5, B-3000 Leuven (Belgium)

ISBN SBN 90 5867 569 6
ISBN 978 90 5867 569 9
D/2006/1869/52
NUR: 652

Final editing: Liesbeth Decan, Rein Deslé, Katelijne Schiltz and Hilde Van Gelder

Translations: Erik Boersma, Rebecca Nuyts and Katelijne Schiltz.

Lay-out: Fran Deslé

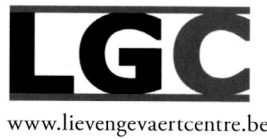

www.lievengeuertcentre.be

Lieven Gevaert Research Centre
Arts Faculty K.U.Leuven
Blijde-Inkomststraat 21
B-3000 Leuven

Hilde Van Gelder (Ed.)

IN THE NAME OF MOZART

Photographs by

MALOU SWINNEN

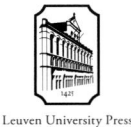

Leuven University Press

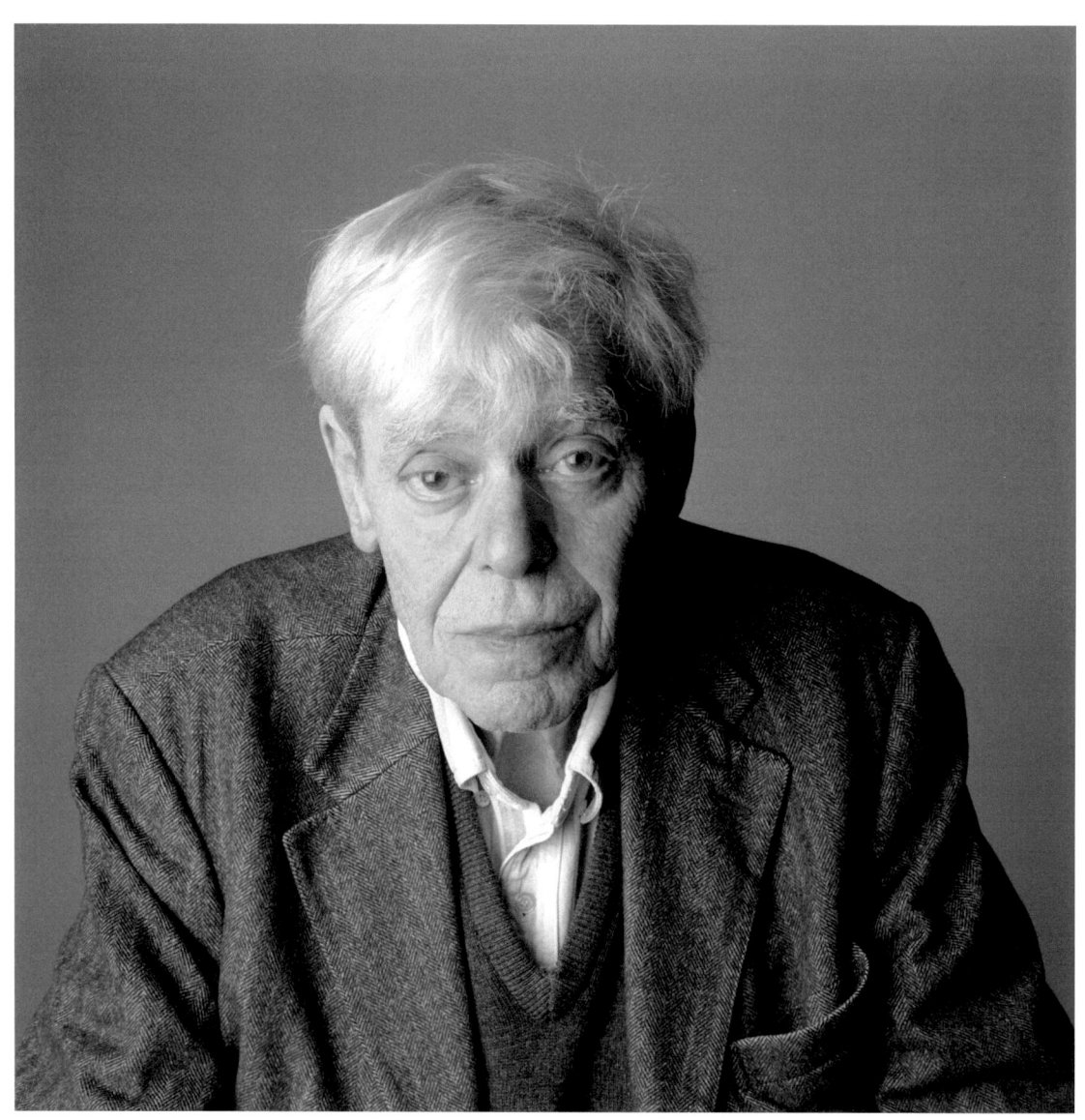

Frans Brüggen

Contents

Preface

'Beauty asks for a permanent, excessive discipline'. So opens the art book 'PERSONAE' by photographer Malou Swinnen. Beauty doesn't come cheaply. It isn't a disposable article or a barcode or a quick snack. As in every work of art, the quest for beauty is related to the quest for the artist's intentions. And this quest is exciting, but demands study, concentration, time and love.

'In the Name of Mozart' has become a testament, centred around the quest of the musician for the master composer, the visual artist for the musician-as-person, the listener for the performer. It is the quest for images and words to express beauty and its permanent presence.

Music, that beating heart in our bodies, directs the other artistic disciplines. The mission of the Concertgebouw as an international centre for performing arts, with a central place given to vocal and instrumental traditions, is to be a laboratory for creation. The quest for creation during Mozart06, our festival last spring, led to 'In the Name of Mozart', the project realised by Malou Swinnen and curator Prof. Dr. Hilde Van Gelder.

> *Regard a candle's flame and see its beauty.*
> *Blink and look again.*
> *What you now see was not there before*
> *And what was there is gone.*
> [Leonardo da Vinci]

Like the flickering of the flame, the creative moment can be infinitely ephemeral, and infinitely beautiful. In its eternity it is burned onto our retinas, into our ear-drums. Allow me to invite you to listen with me to 17 frozen-in-time/hushed/captured portraits, now-moments visualised 'In the Name of Mozart'.

A word of thanks to Malou Swinnen and Prof. Dr. Hilde Van Gelder for the passion, attention to concept and intensity with which they realised this project together with us. In addition, my thanks go out to the 17 musicians portrayed, to the whole staff, to the Lieven Gevaert Research Centre for Photography and Visual Studies, to Leuven University Press and to the KULeuven.

I wish you the pleasure of intense viewing and hushed listening.

Bart Demuyt,
Artistic Director, Concertgebouw Bruges
1 September 2006

Prelude:
The Project 'In the Name of Mozart'

In the Fall of 2005, the Concertgebouw Bruges contacted the Lieven Gevaert Research Centre for Photography and Visual Studies at the University of Leuven (LGC), announcing the challenging proposal to work out a collaborative project with the renowned Belgian portrait photographer Malou Swinnen (°1944). As 2006 in Bruges, like in many other places, was conceived as the 'Mozart year', the idea was that Malou Swinnen would portray a fine selection of those musicians who would find their way to the Concertgebouw during the period of its concert series Mozart06, in order to perform the delightful music of Wolfgang Amadeus Mozart (1756-1791). The resulting portraits would not only constitute an exhibition at the Concertgebouw, but would also be the fundaments of a book, produced in close collaboration between both institutions involved and the artist.

This is the book that you are now holding in your hands. Between February and June 2006, Malou Swinnen held seventeen photo shoots at the Concertgebouw of just as many performers, a few hours before they would go on stage. Previously, she had asked them to bring an attribute to the shoot, which they had selected themselves and which would throw some light on their relationship to Mozart. Thus, with the exception of Frans Brüggen, she photographed all of them twice: one time with their self-selected attributes and one time without them. For the portraits without attributes, the artist asked her models, while being photographed, to think about Mozart, his music or the meaning of his music to them.

Both series have been reproduced in this book. The sixteen portraits without attributes have been reproduced full page and in colour. They are also the ones exhibited in the Concertgebouw Bruges from November 2006 until May 2007. The order in which they appear in this publication, is the order in which they were photographed. The choice to present them here one after the other, in their 'sounding silence', has been a deliberate one. This has been explained more in detail in the first essay which follows directly after this introduction, written by Katelijne Schiltz and myself. In that text, we explore the fascinating yet highly problematic relationship between music and the visual arts, especially photography. Key issue of our concerns is first and foremost the question whether it is possible to 'hear an image' or - the other way around - 'to see music', in particular by means of a score.

Besides that, this project has, from the beginning to the end, become particularly involved in matters of memory and remembrance. Conceived to commemorate the extraordinary musical genius of Wolfgang Amadeus Mozart, Mozart06 now in itself has become a fine memory through Malou Swinnen's photographic portraits of some of its most excellent performers. Now, in the Fall of 2006, recovering Mozart's music and making it come to life, is no longer done by the execution of his most exemplary pieces, but by making them resonate again in the minds and memories of those looking at the pictures of its performers, who were thinking of Mozart at the very moment their image was being fixed. All of them had their own story to tell about Mozart and about what he meant to their musical and personal life. This is reflected in the second group of images that is included in this book, and which have been reproduced in black-and-white, although they were originally in colour. Their commemorative aspect is thus heightened. It is even strengthened by the fact that all performers have agreed to write down a short notice about what Mozart means to them. This has been published underneath their portraits. Malou Swinnen herself has also extensively taken notes after each photo shoot, in order to remember the conversations she had with her models while working with them. For, like every good portrait photographer, Swinnen conceives a photosession as a private and very intense moment between the 'subject' - the photographer - and the 'object' - the photographed person. She rarely or never allows any third person to be present when she is at work and usually follows a strict working pattern.

The second essay in this book, written by Liesbeth Decan, digs into Malou Swinnen's photographic methodology and artistic preoccupations from a historical perspective. Based on an in-depth interview with the artist, this text manages to throw light for the first time on the conditions in which Swinnen's body of work has been established over the years and on the most important points of reference for her career. Using the Hasselblad camera, she can operate quickly in a well-installed studio - which in this case she did in the quiet mezzanine of the musician's lounge at the Concertgebouw. The annotations the artist has made are highly revealing about the way the portrayed models think about Mozart. She has generously put them at my disposal and I therefore rehearse some of them here, but they are best to be read while looking at the pictures from time to time that are included in the last pages of this book. For example, Eric Sleichim explained to Malou Swinnen that he calls his porcelain gnome 'Pim Mozart'. This is meant as a wink at the oeuvre of Mozart, which he feels is full of winks as well. At the same time he sees a nice voltage curve between the choice for this attribute and the performance of that night – the concert *Mozart-Machine* of 28 January 2006 in which he shows the tragic Mozart to the public. Laughs and tears, people hear it all the time in relation to Mozart …

During his conversation with the photographer Sigiswald Kuijken calls Mozart 'profound'. He considers him to be a complete artist, frivolous and terrified at the same time, scabrous and religious. Marcel Ponseele as well as Ton Koopman attach great importance to the field of tension between Mozart as a child prodigy and what kind of traces this has left behind in his later life and in his compositions. Also Olga Pasichnyk has chosen a score of a children's song – the first one she sang as a child – and of a lullaby she sings for her two-year-old son. Claire Chevallier with a smile and twinkling eyes very convincingly shows Malou Swinnen that Mozart is 'the essence' for her. To enforce that enigma, she brought her tuning fork with her.

Erik Vermeulen opted for a small cd, as a symbol for the heavenly transference of sound of which Mozart is capable. Alexei Lubimov is holding the score which he needed for his performance of that evening. He cherishes it like a child would do with its most precious toy, this is the way he explains his choice. The same goes for Melvyn Tan, for whom Mozart corresponds with life itself and the deepest human emotions. Ronald Brautigam, for comparable reasons, brings volume 20 with him from the collected works of Mozart. Midori Seiler shows us a plastic bottle with multivitamins. To her, he is a complete nourishment which 'recharges' her spiritually, physically and emotionally, she tells Malou Swinnen. Jos van Immerseel very suitably chose a key from his pianoforte. The beautiful, graphic object symbolises the three authentic instruments with which he lets Mozart resound to the current public: the pianoforte, the harpsichord and the clavichord.

Jan Michiels is holding a wooden miniature theatre, with three detached little figures in it. He bought it in a shop in Brussels as a gift for his wife and got her permission to bring it with him. He chose it because it symbolises what he sees is the most important element of Mozart's oeuvre: the operas. In these plays all the elements characteristic of Mozart's compositions come together, to him they are a *Gesamtkunstwerk*. Claron McFadden is acting very playfully and tender as if she is taking a bite of a chocolate *Mozartkugel*. To her Mozart is light, childlike, deceptively simple and sometimes a little kitsch. Enchanting delicacies to be consumed, like chocolate.

Roel Dieltiens opts for a special attribute: his wife. He chose her because he, as a result of the pieces he will play that evening, got convinced of the fact that Mozart must have deeply loved his wife. You notice this from the way he wrote the music – namely the *String quintet in c KV 406*, the *Duo for violin and viola in G KV 423* and the *String quintet in D KV 593*, says Dieltiens. Because of this, in the photographic image of man and woman Malou Swinnen chooses to depict the heads intimately close to each other. Very special about this image is the fact her head finds itself just under his, while he puts his hands around her neck. As a result the head receives a disembodied effect like the one of Saint John the Baptist on the plate of Salomé. With this image Malou Swinnen very brightly spots Mozart's relation to women and at the same time represents a striking, more universal image of the man-woman relationship.

Michel Portal brought his clarinet with him, his most precious jewel. He was going to improvise Mozart virtuoso that night. During the recordings he emphasizes the level of difficulty of this, but it is almost as if the instrument he is carrying with him, gives him the strength and self-confidence he needs. Frans Brüggen did not have himself photographed with an attribute. For this reason, his portrait falls 'outside of category' in a certain way. With his glazed eyes he is looking right through us as a 'mother image'. Malou Swinnen's picture of this company's Nestor therefore is an ideal point of departure for the sensitive story that develops through this series of images. Mozart was a master at portraying man in all his facets. This series of photographic portraits made 'in the name of', are a subtle and penetrating homage to his genius and to what he gave the world.

A project of this dimension could not have been realized without the commitment of many people. I especially would like to thank Bart Demuyt, artistic director of the Concertgebouw, for his excellent initiative, for the pleasant, fascinating collaboration and for the confidence he had in us. Without the infinite commitment of Riet Jaeken, Koen Jambon and Yves De Bruyckere of the Concertgebouw Bruges *In the Name of Mozart* would not have become what it is now. Many thanks for this. In the Lieven Gevaert Centre Rein and Fran Deslé meticulously and creatively took care of the logistics and layout of the book respectively. Rebecca Nuyts took excellent care as always of the necessary translations. I thank the co-authors of this book, Katelijne Schiltz and Liesbeth Decan for their interesting contributions. Finally, giving credit where credit is due, this project is dedicated to the artistic work of one exceptional artist, Malou Swinnen. To her goes my deepest gratitude for the nice collaboration, the punctuality and collegiality.

Hilde Van Gelder
Guestcurator *In the Name of Mozart*

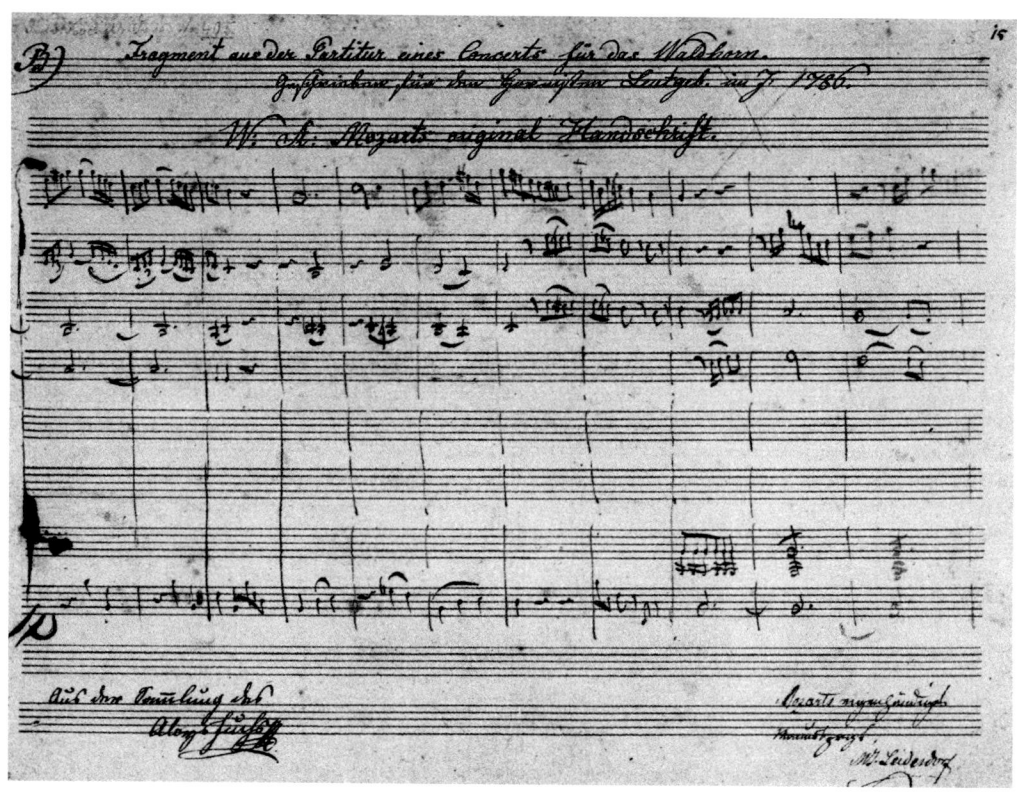

Plate 1: W.A. Mozart, Concerto for Horn in E flat major, KV 495
(with kind permission from The Morgan Library & Museum)

Sounding Silence:
Mozart, Music, and the Visual Arts

Katelijne Schiltz and Hilde Van Gelder

Introduction: a common affinity?

When composers, performers or listeners are talking about music, it is striking to notice how often, either consciously or unconsciously, they are using terms that are first and foremost associated with the visual arts. Whilst for example describing the aural effect of a particular instrument or instrumental combination of an orchestra, one often uses words like *colour* or *warmth*. Tonalities too, are not seldom compared with nuances of *darkness* or *brightness*: major tonalities (having a major third in the tonic) tend to be associated with 'light', while minor tonalities (having a minor third in the tonic) are usually said to be 'dark' (Jewanski 2001, 156-160). Music can also be described in terms of *texture* – a word which etymologically has its origins in the craft of weaving (Lat.: texere). A passage for full orchestra can be said to have a 'full texture', while a passage with reduced instrumental forces (for example a soloist in a concerto) is characterised by a 'thin texture'. A composition can thus often be interpreted as an organic fluctuation in textures. On a more abstract and formal level, a musical piece also has a certain *depth*, as it contains several hierarchically differentiated dimensions and layers, from small recurring motifs and phrases over periods to large-scale forms and movements.

Interestingly enough, in Mozart's lifetime, these similarities and the relation between music and the visual arts were the subject of numerous philosophical and scientific investigations as well as literary outpourings. In his treatise with the highly suggestive title *Ueber die musikalische Malerey* (1780), Johann Jakob Engel discusses exactly the kind of correspondences between the aural and visual impressions we have just described. According to him, similarities do exist between the arts that go beyond the individual senses: 'There are similarities, not only between objects of one sense, but also between objects of different senses. For example, one can find slowness and swiftness in a series of tones as well as in a series of visual impressions. I wish to call all such similarities transcendental similarities'.[1] A few years before Engel's publication, Johann Friedrich Reichardt - Frederick the Great's future chapel-master - had already expanded upon such a remarkable 'Aehnlichkeit' in one of his *Briefe eines aufmerksamen Reisenden die Musik betreffend* (1774-1776). In this piece of writing, he draws a parallel between the composer's use of dynamics (loud or soft) and the painter's use of colours (light or dark). In either case, the meaning can differ according to the particular context: 'Both *forte* and *piano* are in Adagio very different from what they are in Allegro; the painter, similarly, uses very different degrees of light and shade in depicting a sad or gentle situation and in a merry banquet scene or furious battle piece' (Tolley 2001, 144-145).

The discourse on the correspondences between artistic disciplines was of course not initiated during the Age of Enlightenment, since it goes back to much earlier times. In the seventeenth century already, men of science such as Isaac Newton and Athanasius Kircher had developed theories about analogies between music and visual elements in general and colours in particular. In his *Hypothesis Explaining the Properties of Light* (1675), Newton associated the seven colours of the spectrum with the seven principal intervals (from second to octave). This treatise was made accessible to a wider public by Francesco Algarotti: the success of his *Il Newtonianismo per le dame* (1737) is testified by numerous English and German translations. Before Newton, Athanasius Kircher had already presented a system for linking colours and intervals in his *Musurgia universalis* (1650). A similar idea was proposed in Kircher's *Ars magna lucis et umbrae* (1646) in which he even added tables to explain the analogies between notes, colours, intensities of light and degrees of brightness. Perhaps the most famous example of ambitions to create an aesthetic of visual music is Father Castel's *clavecin oculaire* (1729-1754). Father Castel carried out daring experiments, in which he tried to connect musical notes with colours; green for example was made to correspond to *re*. In his opinion, a combination of diverse sensual experiences would produce a much richer artistic experience. In other words, he actually believed a truly kinaesthetic art could be possible.

In the romantic period too, one continued to write about the similarities between music and the visual arts. These are for instance expressed in a rather intuitive way by E.T.A. Hoffmann's Kapellmeister Johannes Kreisler, who is the main figure in many of Hoffmann's stories. He could be considered as the prototype of a 'Künstler' for whom crossing the boundaries between the disciplines and the senses was something natural: 'I find colours, notes and scents all coming together, not so much in a dream as in that state of delirium that precedes sleep, particularly when I have been listening to a great deal of music' (Jewanski 2001, 157).

It seems reasonable to assume that for artists, such as Mozart, seeing and exploring the link between music and the visual arts was more or less self-evident. As several of Mozart's letters reveal, the composer was highly sensitive to visual stimuli. Witness many of his travels with his father Leopold, during which they spent almost as much time admiring works of art as attending concerts. In a letter written on 17 October 1763, we can read about their fascination for the fifteenth-century altarpiece by Dirk Bouts at Saint Peter's Church in Louvain. Two years later, during one of their travels in the Low Countries, father and son must have been deeply touched by Rubens' *Descent from the Cross* in the Antwerp Cathedral, as testifies Leopold's letter of 19 September 1765 (Tolley 2001, 16-17).

Not only Mozart, but other famous composers as well showed a similar interest in the visual arts. Joseph Haydn and Carl Philipp Emanuel Bach were even genuine collectors of works of art. As can be deduced from a catalogue drawn up after his death, Haydn did not only keep paintings from the Old Masters and literary prints, but also caricatures and portraits (Tolley 2001, 324-327). Carl Philipp Emanuel Bach seems to have had a predilection for portraits, especially of his colleague-composers. As the famous Charles Burney witnesses in one of his extensive travel reports, the composer had 'a large and elegant music room, furnished with pictures, drawings and prints of more than a hundred and fifty musicians: among whom, there are many Englishmen, and original portraits, in oil of his father and grandfather' (Scholes 1959, 219). It is thus clear that, from a very early age on, musicians have been particularly attracted to the portrait genre. The birth of the photographic medium in the late 1830s certainly came to fill an important role in this respect. Moreover, ever since photographs of musicians, directors or composers came to illustrate record sleeves, the medium has revolutionised the music industry. Who would not remember Herbert von Karajan's photogenic face on the DG-records?

Contemplating the score

When a director of an orchestra or a choir, an instrumentalist, a singer or a musicologist is studying a score to prepare a performance or an analysis, one could say that several senses are activated simultaneously. To quote the title of a recent book by Cristle Collins Judd (2000), one is 'hearing with the eyes'. Reading a score is a very active matter indeed, through which one tries to bring the music to life by a kind of 'inner ear'. Although the way one reads a score can differ greatly according to each person's skills, goals and intentions, certain typical mechanisms can nevertheless be distinguished. First of all, the eye almost automatically looks for a number of parameters, which are necessary to 'get a picture' of the music as a whole. Attention is focused on crucial elements – which in most cases probably are the very first thoughts the composer himself has put on paper – such as the scoring (Is it a vocal or an instrumental piece? How many parts are involved? Is it intended for a soloist or an ensemble?), the tonality of the piece and the tempo (e.g. allegro or andante). After having stored this information, one starts to 'zoom in' and to perceive more details about the musical 'landscape' by analysing aspects such as formal schemes, the handling of several motifs etc. It is thus possible to distinguish several phases, ranging from general to specific information, from an overall impression to details concerning the structure and the content of the music.

'Reading a score' asks for a very active participation and a capacity of 'inner imagination'. Studying a score is also a silent activity, a characteristic which bears a remarkable resemblance to analysing works of art in general and photographs in particular. A musical score, just like an image, carries a great communicative potential. However, it is clear that not every person is capable of reading such a score and of finding his or her way through the musical landscape. Indeed, musical notation is a code. If one wants to decipher it in order to perform or analyse the music, one needs to know the key to do so.

In the course of music history, musical notation has gradually developed in such a way that composers were more and more able to fix the parameters by means of the written medium: melody, rhythm, tempo, dynamics etc. (Haar 1995, 265-284). Notwithstanding the tendency to render a composer's wishes 'as accurate as possible' – a striving which reached its absolute climax in the twentieth-century serialism, which determines every note exactly and individually in terms of pitch, duration, dynamics etc. – it is interesting to see how the written text allows for quite varying approaches and interpretations: every performance – either live or recorded on CD – is different. Although the notation is by definition the same for everybody, the written text leads directors and musicians to a different 'translation'.[2] Every person thus 'reads' the score in a different way; every written text leads to a very personal imagination. In this respect one can also argue that there are certain similarities between the observation of a score and that of a picture. Besides, as Gotthold Lessing already stated in 1766, the bringing into play of the 'free rein of the imagination' – meaning the add-on by our imagination to what the eye perceives in the moment represented – is necessary to any successful contemplation of a picture as well (Lessing 1984, 19). It is crucial, Lessing argues, that a painting is represented as concise and worked-out as possible, regarding the sole intention that the observer of the piece starts imagining what would happen right after the scene depicted.

The score as objet d'art?

From our point of view, the musical score has a rather paradoxical status. Can the written text possibly be the composer's 'end product' or not? On the one hand: no, because the score still has to be realised by the performers. On the other hand: yes, as the score carries by definition the potential of the audible result. Furthermore, the score is the key, the necessary medium or 'mediating instance' between the composer, the performer(s) and the public. For a composer, the score is the ideal way to preserve his thoughts, to communicate these with musicians and to save his work from being a non-recurring aural event. The fleeting nature of a musical performance is thus countered by the score, which makes the multiplication of performances possible. Despite the suggestion of a certain material permanency or uniqueness of the score, there remains a fundamental difference with the visual arts. Even though, as we have just said, the score is a necessary medium for the composer to communicate with performers, analysts etc., it cannot be considered a work of art as such. One should therefore be cautious about drawing far-reaching analogies between musical scores and visual pictures, paintings and photographs in particular.[3]

What precedes does not imply that scores were never treated with a certain aesthetical consideration in mind. Examples revealing such a concern for the visual presentation of music already go back to the music of the Middle Ages and the Renaissance. Especially pieces with a self-referential character – i.e. compositions with texts that describe the work itself – have been the subject of such visual attention. To name but a few illustrations: the anonymous fourteenth-century ballad *En la maison Dedalus* (about a lover who gets lost in the 'house of Daedalus') is depicted in the form of a labyrinth, as is shown in the manuscript Berkeley [California], University Library, fol. 31ᵛ (Crocker 1967, 161-171). Baude Cordier's *Tout par compas suy compose* (Hoppin 1978, 485) and Jacob de Senleches' *La harpe de mélodie* respectively take the shape of a circle and a harp. Finally, canons by Ludwig Senfl and Adam Gumpelzhaimer were depicted in the form of a cross (Schiltz 2003, 227-256).

During the classical period too, we have some remarkable instances of pieces where the visual attractiveness of a score is given particular attention. Mozart himself left us some fascinating autographs, notated in different colours. A famous example is his Concerto for Horn in E flat major, KV 495 (**plate 1**). The partially incomplete score is notated in four different colours of ink (black, blue, red and green), an idea that was generally supposed to be some kind of joke. More recently, however, it has been suggested that the use of varying colours served the purpose of coding instructions that denote refinements of dynamics and nuances (Giegling 1987, xiii). This way, Mozart's 'colour experiments' could be seen as a technique to convey expressive qualities in the interpretation of the music, which standard notation could not indicate. The colours thus not only give instructions for the performers - indicating nuances such as *sotto voce*, echo, *forte* and *piano* - but they also have a certain analytical quality.

Joseph Haydn too played with colours and forms in some of his compositions. A famous example is *Thy voice o harmony is divine*, which he submitted for his doctoral degree from the University of Oxford in July 1791 (see **plate 2** for a transcription). In one of the autographs, the work – consisting of several retrograde and inversion canons – has been represented in the form of a circle, the ultimate symbol for God's being without beginning and without end. Apart from that, Haydn used different colours of ink to indicate how the voices should read the music. Canons in general seem to have been Haydn's main field for experimenting with forms and other visual clues. As we can read in the inventory of Haydn's artistic possessions drawn up after his death, he even appears to have used a series of canons (mainly based on German texts) as wall paintings ('Bilder') in his study room. Mozart's widow Konstanze confirms in a letter written on 23 December 1809 that she herself has seen these pieces (Deutsch 1959, vii and 1932-33, 112-114). So, as Thomas Tolley puts it: 'The trouble Haydn went to in framing and displaying these manuscripts implies a recognition to this type of composition that a certain aesthetic pleasure might be derived from *looking* at the scores, as well as from *listening* to their music' (Tolley 2001, 208).

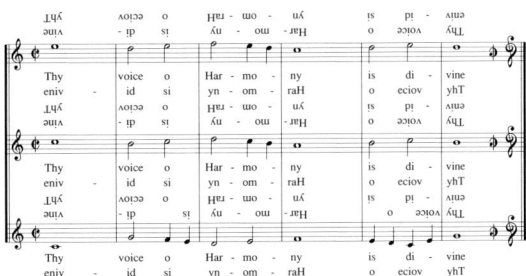

Plate 2: *Joseph Haydn, Thy Voice o Harmony is Divine* (with kind permission of Henle Verlag)

Music, the score and communication

As we have stated above, the musical score holds communicative potential, provided one knows the code and knows how to read and interpret the signs. In the course of the eighteenth century, several scholars from various disciplines have seriously and fundamentally questioned exactly this 'problem' (Klotz 2000, 306-338). In his treatise *Neues Organon oder Gedanken über die Erforschung und Bezeichnung des Wahren und dessen Unterscheidung vom Irrthum und Schein. Zweyter Band. Semiotik oder Lehre von der Bezeichnung der Gedanken und Dinge* (1764), scientist Johann Heinrich Lambert, for example, criticised the visual deficiency of musical notation. He complained about the fact that one cannot 'see' the syntactical connection between the notes, hence whether a chord or interval is consonant or dissonant. One can only judge when the signs are studied, so that one can read, play or compose music. Other scholars tried to remedy this problem by developing alternative systems for notating music. About twenty years before Lambert's book, Jean-Jacques Rousseau published his ambitious *Projet concernant de nouveaux signes pour la musique* (1742), in which he proposed a new system of music notation. What he did was replacing the notes by numbers, so that everybody could see the connections between the signs.[4] The project was, however, no big success: Rousseau's notation was not capable of including the semantic density of the music, which in fact only increased the distance between deciphering and reading the signs. Another problem of Rousseau's project was the fact that his system was not able to visualise the emotional impact of music. A third key figure in this overview of critiques dismissing the traditional notation of music is Carl Philipp Emanuel Bach. His main objection was the presence of bar lines in the score. According to him, bar lines hamper the performer's free expression of feelings. As he puts it in his *Versuch über die wahre Art das Clavier zu spielen* (1753): 'Fantasising without bar lines seems especially appropriate for the expression of "Affekte", because each bar line has a kind of constraint. The bar is thus often used because of the notational convention, but one is not necessarily tied to it' (Bach 1753, 124).[5] Bach's ideal was a music without bar lines, something he realised in his *Freye Fantasie fis-moll*. Operating his system, Bach invited the performer to fill in the emotional shortcomings of the notation and to communicate his feelings with the listeners.

Hearing music through pictures

In his *Versuch über die wahre Art das Clavier zu spielen*, Carl Philipp Emanuel Bach presents some other extremely interesting thoughts, namely about how the performer – similar to an actor – should share his emotions with his public. More specifically, Bach elaborates on the way a musician's body language in general and his facial expression in particular have to mirror his emotional state, which should be communicated towards the audience.[6] It is striking that many Mozart performers photographed by Malou Swinnen, possess that particular kind of bodily language: we vividly recall the Kuijken brothers' agitated yet controlled upper body's movements (to the point of saliva dropping out of Barthold Kuijken's transverse flute on the floor when he opened it on stage), even if they were sitting on a chair. Their was a tremendous synergy between these player-members of the same family, who know each other so long and so well. It did remind one of those wonderful stories of Mozart and his sister Nannerl playing the piano not only when they were children, but even at a later age.[7] The Kuijkens transferred their tremendous joy of playing to the public, evoking an atmosphere as intimate as if they were sitting in a living room. This reflects how completely geared up they are to each other. No less fascinating was, for example, the masterful bodily synergy between the soprano Olga Pasichnyk and the pianist Claire Chevallier while they brought some of Mozart's *Lieder* in a highly intimate, female way: it was a receptive yet strong and firm, and extremely warm performance. Unforgettable are Midori Seiler's straight back and shoulders while playing the violin or Jos van Immerseel's movements of the head while being completely immersed in his execution of Mozart's pianoconcertos. Still, by far the most remarkable was the explosion of bodily energy springing from Frans Brüggen's acts of direction. Seated on a chair, his outstretched arms and enormous hands flew through the air as merciless swords. The orchestra – as much as the public – only had eyes for him: it was a moment of magical synergy.

Carl Philipp Emanuel Bach's ideas about the importance of the body's communicative potential can also be situated against the background of the eighteenth-century discourse on the relationship between somebody's outer appearance and inner being. Johann Kaspar Lavater was especially known for his research on this field. In his *Physiognomische Fragmente* (4 volumes, 1775-1784), Lavater seeks a scientific justification for the correspondences between a person's visual appearance and his or her creative personality (Mraz 1996, 165-176). He introduced the notion that facial features, formations of the body, and even characteristics of handwriting were visual manifestations of the individual's inner character. Lavater seems to have been interested especially in the face as a mirror of the inner being. Not coincidentally, he possessed a collection of portrait silhouettes, on which his studies were partially based.

A similar concept was pursued and put into practice by the sculptor Franz Xaver Messerschmidt, who made a series of so-called 'Charakterköpfe' **(plate 3)**. Each male bust represented a different state of mind (such as 'troubled', 'melancholic', 'cheerful' etc.). In 1759, the French *Académie* had already instituted a 'prix d'expression' for the study of heads in expressions of emotion. This idea was probably also favoured by the Viennese *Akademie*, where Messerschmidt was working as a teacher. It is very likely that Joseph Haydn knew about Messerschmidt's 'Köpfe'. As we have said in the above, the composer himself also kept a series of portraits, especially from composers and musicians such as Antonio Salieri and the singer Anna Morichelli (Tolley 2001, 164). Apparently, such portraits possessed a highly suggestive character, as can be judged from another interesting witness too. It is told how during a performance of an oratorio by Carl Philipp Emanuel Bach in 1789, organised by Baron von Swieten at the residence of Prince Johann Esterházy, a portrait of the composer was passed around the audience. The main purpose of this initiative seemed apparently to enable the audience to equate characteristics of the music with features of the composer's appearance.

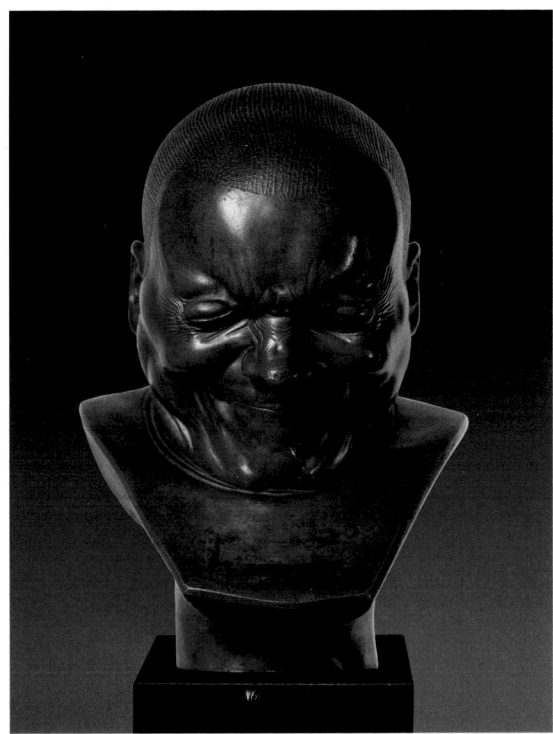

Plate 3: Franz Xaver Messerschmidt, *Ein Erzbösewicht* (Nr. 33 aus der Folge der «Charakterköpfe»), nach 1770, with kind permission of the Österreichische Galerie Belvedere.

A glance through the program of *Mozart06* reveals the current application of this strategy of incorporating pictures of composers, divas and star performers into the presentation brochure, in order to attract the potentially interested public. Except for Frans Brüggen and Michel Portal, the brochure contains all Mozart performers portrayed later on by Malou Swinnen in full-page shots, serving as 'photographic bait'. The images range from frontal busts to profiles, from full-length portraits to quasi-details of the face. Most musicians in the leaflet do not look into the lens. Right from the beginning, Malou Swinnen, by contrast, chose to steer a much more rigid course. Besides opting systematically for the square picture form of the *Hasselblad* camera, she treated all her models the same by consistently placing them right in front of the lens against a solid grey background and by asking them to peer straight into the lens while thinking of Mozart. The camera angle cut the image at bust height, mercilessly.

In this book and the exhibition as well, all the pictures align and have equal size, which creates a strong juxtaposing effect. In the *Concertgebouw*, these large-format images offer the additional impression of being confronted with some kind of contemporary iconostasis. The music, which is internalised by the models and which can be told from their photographed faces, is pseudo-divine and represents itself as thoughts of angel's voices.

The 'acoustic image'

The shots of Malou Swinnen can be regarded as an instantaneous photograph of interior 'involvement' with music in general and with Mozart in particular. In a highly exceptional, tranquil and interiorised way each artist-performer expresses his or her creative act to the photographer, straight before it will take place. This manner, the image transcends its merely visual character and becomes almost 'audible'. In this respect w.j.t. Mitchell justly writes about an 'acoustic image', which he defines as an image that is able to 'pass over the boundary between vision and hearing' (Mitchell, 2005, 2). Swinnens photographs that make up *In The Name of Mozart* indeed want to be "*heard*" (Mitchell, 2005, 45), as Mitchell argues: they appear to express the explicit desire of not wanting to be silent or still.

Each picture at hand bears this kind of 'acoustic potential': the facial expression of the performer announces the musical atmosphere in which (s)he, together with the public, will be plunged a few hours later. In the remarks noted down after the shootings and during the conversations we had about this matter, Malou Swinnen provides clarifying information. For instance, while Malou Swinnen made Sigiswald Kuijken's portrait-without-attribute, both Kuijken's hands were lying on top of two red volumes that he had brought and that belong to the collected works of Mozart. The books are not brought into vision at all, since the photographer pitilessly cut out all but the bust. Still, the knowledge that Kuijken was searching 'energy' via the scorings through his hands while he was looking right into the lens, thinking of Mozart, adds a deeper dimension to the image which we eventually get to see. After the photo session, this terribly talented performer of Mozart notified that his secretive act of touching the books really did cause music of Mozart to sound in his head while being photographed, which he imitated aloud: "pompompompom...".

Also Ton Koopman claimed firmly that one specific tone of the concert that he was playing later that evening, resonated in his head when being photographed. Claire Chevallier too thought of songs that she was about to accompany that evening on the pianoforte: playful songs, but also serious ones, among other things about an aging woman who complains about the behaviour of men. Midori Seiler acknowledges that she finds Mozart quite difficult to play because his music is so 'misleadingly simple'. She prepares herself for an effortless performance of Mozart's subtlety, in which she will succeed masterly. When Michel Portal was next to be photographed, he sang Mozart.

From a retrospective standpoint - meaning, when we look at these pictures nowadays – this aural or acoustic impression has only fortified. This is the case especially for those who attended the concert, because then, not only the musical recollection while contemplating these photos comes into play – at the end one can hum the music while enjoying the images – but also the visual memory of the performance becomes vivid again. One recalls the clothes worn by the performers during their rendering; one looks back to their movements and their complete projection into their role. It is exactly in this respect that Malou Swinnen's series *In The Name of Mozart* approaches very closely certain photographic sensitivities that she has already been carrying along in her work since she started to photograph intensively in the mid '80s. By this we aim at this international group of artist-photographers who, building on the achievements of the use of the photographic medium within the Body Art and the Performance Art of the '70s, are currently better known as the Pictures Generation.[8]

Concerning this matter, Cindy Sherman is the first to think of and in the context of *In The Name of Mozart* this reference is definitely at its place. Sherman is well-known for her staged photographic portrait collections made of and by herself (and in this respect she is differing fundamentally from the work of Malou Swinnen) in which costumes fill a crucial role. Parallel with Sherman, the models portrayed by Malou Swinnen are 'dressed up': they have made themselves up for the performance of that evening. The dress codes that we can perceive, are in line with the expectations one can have of a musical performer. With the exception of Marcel Ponseele maybe, who is wearing a nice, jeansblue, jacket-like shirt, which he will keep on anyway that evening. During the photo shoot, he tells Malou Swinnen that he always wears such a shirt and additionally he states that the clothes a performer wears during a concert – like a suit, a dinner jacket or a cocktail dress – are nothing but working clothes, just like an overall. An aspect that he wants to accentuate.

Malou Swinnen stems from a generation of photographers who was second to none at picturing a social group – of course one thinks firstly of Robert Mapplethorpe or Nan Goldin. Photographers like these make arresting portrays – or *Charakterköpfe* – of which coded collective similarities as well as the subtle, individual accents put by each of these characters, are strikingly brought into vision.

Although she often worked with black-and-white, Malou Swinnen does not eschew to colour her photos. Making use of the frontal directness of a police photo, she has the portrayed subjects shine in their personal beauty. She does not euphemise, nor does she offend her models. She gets the best out of them and shows their true colours. In order to succeed, a rapid pace of work is of vital importance. This functions as one of the materials for her working method, something her annotations about the manner she portrayed Erik Vermeulen reveal indeed: 'We take the photographs at a brisk pace so that movement is involved which prevents the picture from being too tense or static. They have to come across a bit light-hearted, just like the music of Mozart.'

Photography and speed, a remarkable fusion it is, when looking at Malou Swinnen's images. Although they do not quite resemble a snapshot, still, the dynamics of the shooting process is crucial to her: she opts for a minimal and (in her oeuvre) recurrent staging – the series *Young and Beautiful* (2001) may illustrate this well – but once the stage has been set, the shooting of the photographs has to go at high-speed. This process establishes a particular field of tension with the musical image connotations of the pictures themselves. Music asks time in order to be performed and afterwards the performance is irreversibly over. Snapping a photo by contrast – at least in this specific case – does not take much time. Although it attains afterwards some kind of eternity; it changes as it were into an infinite moment of contemplation.

This way, a terrific pendulous swing is created between photography and music. The point at which the two find or touch each other, remains – as we have already said in the above – in the memory: the musician depicted anticipates mentally his or her approaching performance; the spectator hears the very same music, now irrevocably in the past, but reverberating at the sight of these masterly photos.

[1] 'Es giebt nehmlich Aehnlichkeiten, nicht bloß zwischen Gegenständen einerley Sinnes, sondern auch verschiedener Sinne, Langsamkeit und Geschwindigkeit z. B. finden sich eben so in einer Folge von Tönen, als in einer Folge von sichtbaren Eindrücken. Ich will alle dergleichen Aehnlichkeiten transcendentelle Aehnlichkeiten nennen': Johann Jakob Engel, *Ueber die musikalische Malerey*, Berlin 1780, 9 (Klotz 2000, 327).

[2] The same goes also for an analytical approach towards the score. This question was the topic of a recent discussion about 'Critical Reading and Performance Practice' on the e-mail discussion list of the American Musicological Society (ams).

[3] Recently, that critique has convincingly been uttered in Simon Shaw Miller's review of the anthology *Visual Music: Synaesthesia in Art and Music Since 1900* (London 2005). Miller argues that studying the idea of visual music needs an 'explicit, interdisciplinary methodology' and should beware of superficial understanding of such a complex notion as synaesthesia: S. Shaw Miller, 'Visual Music and the Case for Rigorous Thinking', *The Art Book* 13/1 (February 2006), 3-5.

[4] '[…] leur harmonie et leurs accords seroient connus par la seule inspection de signes': Rousseau, *Projet* (1742), 17.

[5] 'Das Fantasiren ohne Tackt scheint überhaupt zu Ausdrückung der Affeckten besonders geschickt zu seyn, weil jede Tackt-Art eine Art von Zwang mit sich führt. […] Der Tackt ist alsdenn offt bloß der Schreib-Art wegen vorgezeichnet, ohne daß man hieran gebunden ist'.

[6] 'Indem ein Musickus nicht anders rühren kan, er sey dann selbst gerührt; so muß er nothwendig sich selbst in alle Affecten setzen können, welche er bey seinen Zuhörern erregen will; er giebt ihnen seine Empfindungen zu verstehen und bewegt sie solchergestalt am besten zur Mitempfindung' (Dahlhaus 1998, 28).

[7] See in this respect, among others, Glover 2005, 9-99.

[8] Cf. also the historical references in the contribution of Liesbeth Decan further on in this book (From *Faces & Fascinations* (1985) to *Cet obscur objet…* (2005). On the Oeuvre of Malou Swinnen).

BIBLIOGRAPHY

BACH, Carl Philipp Emanuel, *Versuch über die wahre Art das Clavier zu spielen*, Berlin 1753.

COLLINS JUDD, Cristle, *Reading Renaissance Music Theory: Hearing with the Eyes* (Cambridge Studies in Music Theory 14), Cambridge 2000.

CROCKER, Richard L., 'A New Source for Medieval Music Theory', *Acta Musicologica* 39 (1967), 161-171.

DAHLHAUS, Carl, *Klassische und romantische Musikästhetik*, Laaber 1998.

DEUTSCH, Otto Erich, 'Haydns Kanons', *Zeitschrift für Musikwissenschaft* 15 (1932-1933), S. 112-124.

DEUTSCH, Otto Erich (ed.), *Kanons* (*Joseph Haydn. Werke*, 31), München-Duisburg 1959.

GIEGLING, Franz (ed.), *Konzerte* (*Neue Ausgabe sämtlicher Werke*, Serie, Werkgruppe 14, Band 5), Kassel etc. 1987.

GLOVER, Jane, *Mozart's Women: His Family, His Friends, His Music*, London 2005.

GUTMAN, Robert W., *Mozart: A Cultural Biography*, New York-San Diego-London 1999.

HAAR, James, 'Music as Visual Language', in Irving Lavin (ed.), *Meaning in the Visual Arts: Views from the Outside. A Centennial Commemoration of Erwin Panofsky (1892-1968)*, Princeton 1995, 265-284.

HOPPIN, Richard H., *Medieval Music*, New York 1978.

JEWANSKI, Jörg, 'Colour and Music', in Stanley Sadie and John Tyrrell (eds.), *The New Grove Music of Music and Musicians*, vol. 6, London 2001, 156-160.

KLOTZ, Sebastian, 'Tonfolgen und die Syntax der Berauschung. Musikalische Zeichenpraktiken 1738-1788', in Inge Baxman, Michael Franz, and Wolfgang Schäffner (eds.), *Das Laokoon-Paradigma. Zeichenregime im 18. Jahrhundert*, Berlin 2000, 306-338.

LESSING, Gotthold E., *Laocoön: An Essay on the Limits of Painting and Poetry* [1766], transl. from the German, with an introd. and notes by E.A. Mc Cormick, Baltimore, London 1984.

MITCHELL, William J.T., *What Do Pictures Want? The Lives and Loves of Images*, London 2005.

MRAZ, Gerda, 'Musikerportraits in der Sammlung Lavater', in Otto Biba and David Wyn Jones (eds.), *Studies in Music History Presented to H.C. Robbins Landon on his Seventieth Birthday*, London 1996, 165-176.

SCHOLES, Percy A. (ed.), *Dr Burney's Musical Tours in Europe*, vol. 2: *An Eighteenth-Century Musical Tours in Central Europe and the Netherlands*, London 1959.

RABINOWITZ, Rea E., *Meaning and Structure in the Visual Arts and Music*, Ph.D. Brandeis University 1974.

SCHILTZ, Katelijne, 'La storia di un'iscrizione canonica tra Cinquecento e inizio Seicento: il caso di *Ad te, Domine, levavi animam meam* di Philippus de Monte (1574)', *Rivista italiana di Musicologia* 38 (2003), 227-256.

SOLOMON, Manyard, *Mozart: A Life*, New York 1995.

STEPHENSON, David Hanford, *On the Visual Representation of Music*, Ph.D. University of Maryland College Park 1988.

SWINNEN, Malou, Unpublished Notes about the making of the Series *In the Name of Mozart*, put at disposal of the authors (January-June 2006).

TOLLEY, Thomas, *Painting the Cannon's Roar: Music, the Visual Arts and the Rise of an Attentive Public in the Age of Haydn, c.1750 to c.1810*, Aldershot etc. 2001.

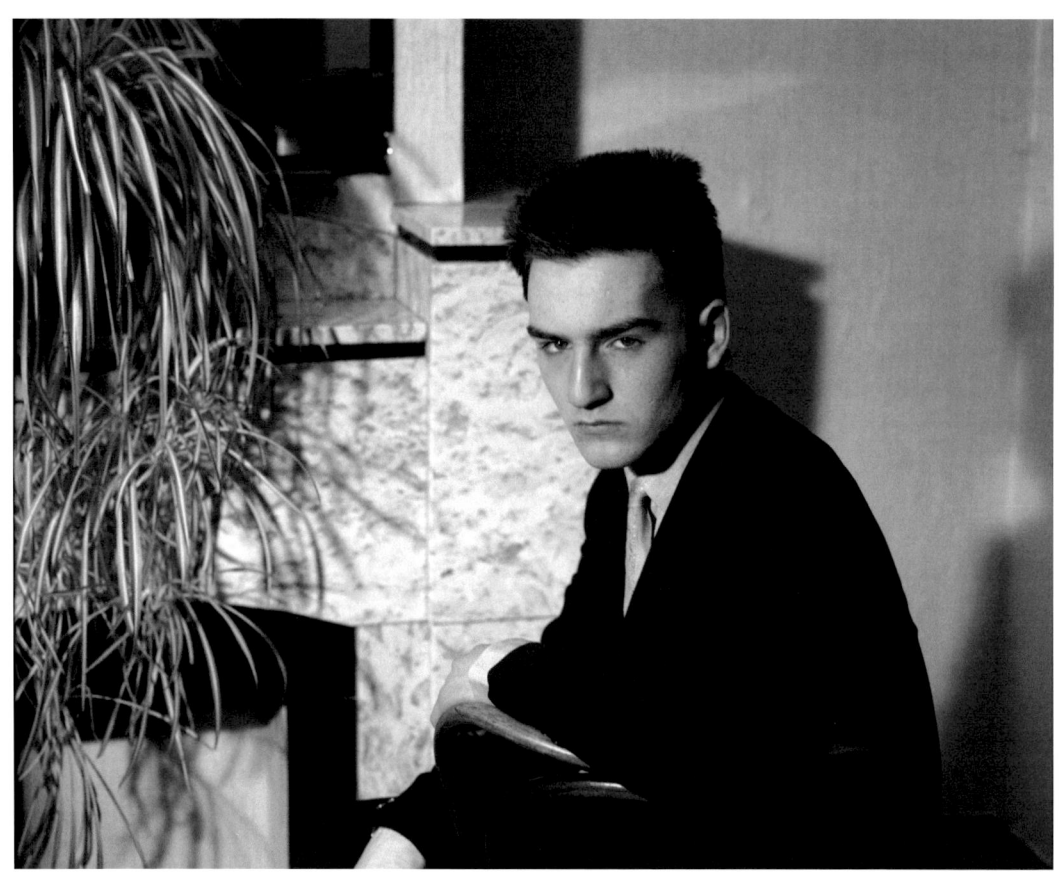

Malou Swinnen, *Untitled*, from the series *Faces & Fascinations*, 1985, c-print, 23 x 28 cm

From *Faces & Fascinations* (1985) to *Cet obscur objet...* (2005)
On the Oeuvre of Malou Swinnen

Liesbeth Decan

The oeuvre of Malou Swinnen embraces a period of twenty years. Reasons enough to have a closer look at her photographic work and to situate it in a contemporary Belgian and international artistic context. At the base of this essay is an interview with the artist, which took place on the 14th of July 2006 in Hasselt. Excerpts of this conversation have been included in this text.

A debut in colour

Each time there is the same young man, handsome, dressed in a classic or rather casual suit, quite satisfied with his looks, a stern face, the whole setting dramatized by a nervous shadowy atmosphere but tempered by a warm colour palette. There is also this sinewy young woman with a bony face (a dancer, so it seems), her hair still wet (after a performance or a training?), bent forward sitting on a black chair against a light background and looking straight into the camera. With these images, portraits of her eldest, then seventeen-year-old son, his friends and girlfriends, or strangers she met in the street or in a bar, Malou Swinnen made her debut in photography. They were exhibited in 1985, entitled *Faces & Fascinations*, in the Stedelijke Academie voor Schone Kunsten in Hasselt. Immediately after that, in 1986, she got the opportunity to show new work in the Provinciaal Museum voor Actuele Kunst (Hasselt). That's how *Kleurenportretten* emerged, building on the theme of the first pictures but metaphorically more accurate and with more glamour. Her fascination for the face and its imperfect beauty has remained the essence of her photographic work.

Malou Swinnen: *"In 1979 I started studying photography at the academy of Hasselt, a study which had been introduced there only four years earlier. My teacher – and from that moment on my mentor for many years - was René Borzée, a former student of Valeer Vanbekbergen at the St Lukas College of Arts in Brussels. Though my artistic choices were quite different from his (he mainly concentrated on the naked body situated in nature, while I preferred to focus on the face and on an intimate inner space like the photo studio), he has always fully supported me. He also introduced me to Jean-Claude Lemagny of the Bibliothèque Nationale de France, who showed me the portfolios of famous photographers like Diane Arbus and later commented on my work. After my studies I tried to show my portfolio to as many professionals as possible: Pool Andries of the Provinciaal Museum voor Fotografie in Antwerp, Alain D'Hooghe, editor in chief of the photography magazine 'Clichés', Karel Van Deuren who wrote for the Dutch 'Foto', Urbain Mulkers of the Provinciaal Museum voor Actuele Kunst in Hasselt (now Z33), etc.*

These people really supported me and this way I got acquainted with the photo scene, I got a chance to exhibit and critics were writing about my work."

The fact that Malou Swinnen had received an education at the municipal academy is characteristic of the almost euphoric climate which has surrounded photography since the end of the 1970s and especially in the beginning of the 1980s in the U.S.A. and in Europe. As for Belgium the continuously growing attention for the medium expressed itself in the foundation of two photographic museums (in Charleroi and Antwerp), numerous photography departments in art colleges and academies,[1] the Espace Photographique Contretype (Brussels) and several photo galleries like Galerie Paule Pia in Antwerp, XYZ in Ghent and 't Pepertje in Diepenbeek, who next to internationally renowned photographers have offered a stage to mainly Belgian photographers (Sarlet 1993: 308 – D'Hooghe 1993: 313). Finally there were also some photo magazines whether or not linked to these galleries, such as Lens en mens, XYZ, 't Pepertje and Clichés (Salu 1993: 271). Though the 'photography-boost' of that period was a general international phenomenon, the Belgian state reforms of 1970 and 1980 also need to be pointed out as contributory causes.

As a result of the federalisation in which Culture became a matter of separate communities, both cultural entities felt the need to affirm their identity – in this case through photography. The Flemish and French Community invested in art studies and also began to collect meticulously. This way the Flemish Community bought some of Malou Swinnen's *Kleurenportretten* in 1986 and in 1996 they bought five portraits from *Personae*. The federalisation, however, also involved the fact that Dutch speaking and French speaking artists, financially dependent on the Flemish and Walloon circuit respectively, were (and are) moving further away from each other.[2] In this respect it is also remarkable the way in which Malou Swinnen – because of her location in Hasselt which is close to Liège and Charleroi – did manage to keep close contact with the Walloon photo scene.

Malou Swinnen: *"Except for Hasselt where besides the Cultural Centre I often frequented the Museum voor Actuele Kunst and Galerie CIAP, I mainly visited exhibitions in the Museum voor Fotografie in Antwerp, Contretype in Brussels, XYZ in Ghent and 't Pepertje in Diepenbeek. Through the photo gallery of the Cultural Centre in Hasselt and through the academy I also got in contact with a lot of Walloon photographers, whose exhibitions I went to visit in Liège and Charleroi. I knew Georges Vercheval, museum director of the Musée de la Photographie in Charleroi, Hubert Grooteclaes, Jean Janssis, Lucia Rodochonska, Jean-Louis Vanesch, Daniel Brunemer and Gilbert Fastenaekens. I also went to the Stedelijk Museum in Amsterdam, where I saw the Robert Mapplethorpe exhibition in 1988."*

Malou Swinnen's profound knowledge of the local contemporary photo scene makes her own artistic choices all the more special. After all, her debut photographs from 1985-86 in many ways deviated from the codes belonging to the then common 'creative photography'. The latter implied black-and-white images with higher contrasts, far-reaching light and shadow effects, the adaptation of the negatives or interventions in the printing process – techniques, with which photography wanted to manifest itself as an artistic form of expression next to the other, more traditional media.

Against this, Swinnen's not manipulated colour shots of young people who almost shamelessly pose in a typical pop outfit, with striking make-up, luxuriant eighties hair and unshaved armpits (the last taboo!), are rebellious. Though other Belgian photographers within this 'artistic/creative photography' were working in colour as well at that time – think of the flower still lives of Paola Ahn, the polaroid compositions of Stefaan De Jaeger, the stagings of Ludo Geysels, some film stills of Toni Geirlandt, certain interiors of Mark De Fraeye or the *Madame*-series of Ria Pacquée – it is, however, quite remarkable the way Malou Swinnen applies the technique of colour photography in order to realize 'pure studio portraits'. Here the directness of the image prevails and not the through manipulation intended 'slowing down' or 'obstruction' in the reading of the image (Andries 1988: n.p.).

The pictures from *Faces & Fascinations* and *Kleurenportretten* do not so much link up with the Belgian context, but rather with an international movement which revolves around the artists of the Pictures Generation, named after the exhibition *Pictures* organized in 1977 by Douglas Crimp in the New York Artists Space. They belong to a movement created around 1960 by artists such as Robert Rauschenberg, Richard Hamilton, Andy Warhol, Ed Ruscha and the happening artists, where photography no longer finds itself in a separate niche (the 'art photography') opposing plastic arts, but is rather used as an artistic medium to realize works of art with (Van Gelder 1995: 20-34).

Malou Swinnen: *"I got most of my inspiration from films. As a matter of fact, film was the immediate cause for me to start working with photography, but instead of the moving image I preferred stills. Films of Visconti, like 'Death in Venice' (1971), where themes such as bourgeois mentality, pose, masquerade and beauty and decline are important. Hitchcock too, with 'Vertigo' (1958) about disguise and adopting a different identity. Also the use of colours in these films from the 1950s drew my attention. Furthermore I think of Ridley Scott's 'Blade Runner' (1982) where I became fascinated with the idea of replicas, or the films of Josef Von Sternberg such as 'Der Blaue Engel' (1930) and 'Morocco' (1930) where Marlene Dietrich plays the androgynous type. Nevertheless, I did not want to make any film stills, but rather portraits of the cast members of 'my' film. These portraits are kinds of glamorous pictures, but with small imperfections so you can still see the stars are ordinary people. I want them to represent my ideas about beauty, but at the same time they should show their own personality.*

Another source of inspiration were the music videos which appeared in the beginning of the 1980s with the foundation of MTV, spreading contemporary music and pop culture in an experimental way. To me, they were also the immediate cause for using colour filters. But apart from moving images (portrait)-painting has been of crucial importance for the development of my metaphorical language. More in particular 15th century Flemish painting, Italian early Renaissance artists like Piero della Francesca, romanticists like Rossetti and symbolist artists like Khnopff.

Why pictures of my eldest son? I found him attractive, photogenic, in my eyes the physical epitome of the Western masculine beauty. He reminded me of movie stars like James Dean, Marlon Brando, Paul Newman, Robert De Niro. And let's not forget: he is me! He is doing exactly the same thing as every female model who is taking my place in front of the camera."

The use of colours, clever poses, striking 'attributes' (make-up, jewellery, gloves, tiger prints) and the above mentioned influence of film and painting links the debut work of Malou Swinnen with the early work of Cindy Sherman, chosen by Crimp as one of the 'picture-makers' (Crimp 1979: 80). Especially Sherman's *Rear Screen Projections* (1980), in which a female character was represented each time against a projected, mostly urban scenery, and *Centrefolds/Horizontals* (1982), in which the protagonist fills the projection surface in a quite artificial pose, are similar as far as the image formation and use of colour are concerned. With the exception of her son and some of his friends, the models in Swinnen's images are always women, mostly represented alone, in close up with minimal scenery surrounding the face and the bust (a plump, soft blanket, a cool sun shade, damp wallpaper). The same basic elements can be found with Sherman, though the dramatic nature wielded by the poses and expressions of the characters – each time performed by Sherman herself – is a lot more manifest. In contrast with this literal cinematographic way of staging, Swinnen's compositions are very austere, also pure and less theatrical.

Still, there is for example a fierceness ensconcing in the showy clothes worn by Swinnen's models, which the seemingly timeless outfits of Sherman do not share. With Swinnen no fictive characters, but 'real' contemporary persons in their own clothes, made up in their own way, in a pose directed only very delicately by the photographer.

This showing of contemporary culture is a component which Swinnen's images share with the famous work of Nan Goldin. Though Goldin's pictures of herself, her friends and her direct surroundings rather have their origins in a reportage reflex and basically have not been staged, some portraits from around 1980 do show some resemblance with the ones belonging to Swinnen: one, sometimes two figures in their own clothes and with their own make-up, showing half their body and in colour. Just like Swinnen (and Sherman) now Goldin seems to be influenced by film as well: the Hollywood diva films of the 1930s-40s, the work of Fellini, Truffaut and Antonioni and the underground films of Jack Smith and Andy Warhol (Weinberg 2005: 14). With Warhol, Swinnen shares the conviction that there is nothing but surface, that it is impossible to fully know and depict someone.

Unlike Swinnen, Goldin does not wait until her characters are in the right position. But the greatest difference between both artists probably lies in the fact that – even when Swinnen is portraying her own son – there is no tangible personal connection between the photographer and the model. Swinnen concentrates on looks, appearance, a principle that is more connected with fashion photography.

The woman's portrait explored in depth

From the beginning Swinnen's attention went exclusively to the portrait genre. While having broken the mould with *Faces & Fascinations* and *Kleurenportretten*, since 1986 she has been zooming in more and more on the classic portrait tradition and especially wishes to perform further research on woman's portraits.

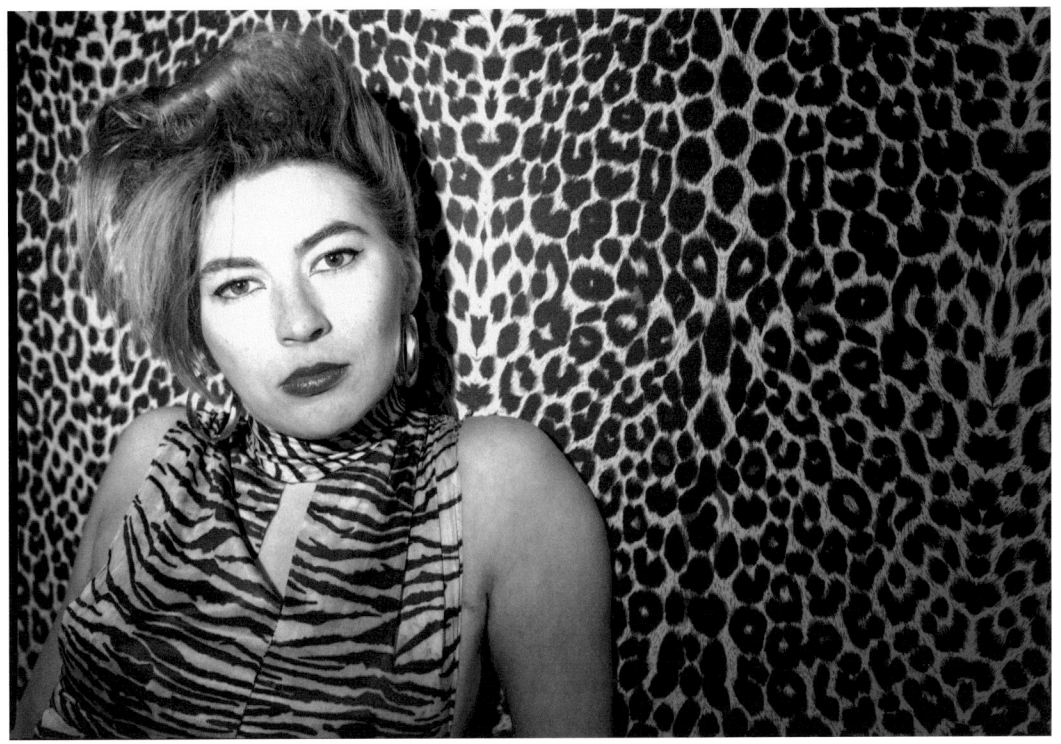

Malou Swinnen, *Untitled*, from the series *Kleurenportretten*, 1986, c-print, 40 x 50 cm

Malou Swinnen: *"After my trip to colour photography I wanted to return to the essence of photography and refine my technique by means of black-and-white photography. From my fascination for the photographic surface of the black-and-white fine print, I started longing again for the aesthetics and the materiality of the traditional medium of photography. During my basic training I already became very influenced by Edward Weston and his interpretation of beauty. Richard Avedon certainly cannot be left out, especially his portraits of the 1950s in which he places the person against a neutral background and thus emphasizes the special trait of that person. I also share his conviction that the vision of the photographer matters. Furthermore, the work of Robert Mapplethorpe also appeals to me because of the aesthetics in the representation of the skin and also the sculptural aspect of his images."*

A period of almost ten years of intensive research – with some exhibitions in Eindhoven, Prague, Hasselt and Brussels – resulted in the book *Personae* in 1995. We repeatedly see a young woman, usually naked, depicted up till her waist, provided with an attribute: a (semi)transparent veil, a mask, pearls, pieces of fake fur, branches of ivy, a thong. The idea of masquerade and pose, seen with Visconti, reappears. The depiction of the skin is Swinnen's primary concern.[3] Not the perfect skin but a real one with freckles, wrinkles, scars and hair. The fine, sensual beauty obtained in spite of, or exactly because of these small imperfections, evokes reminiscences to the *Nudes* of

Edward Weston of the 1920s-30s, though Weston concentrates more on (the curves of) the female body and less on the face. Swinnen speaks via her models' faces. She emphasizes their particularity, but bends them to her will by directing them in a very subtle way. Another aspect of the series is the androgyny - for example to be found in the combination of breasts and hairy arms on the cover image of the book - which provides a dynamic tension to the image and asks questions about the conventional characteristics, codes and roles. In this respect *Personae* involuntarily reminds us of the series *Modern Lovers* (1989-90) of the French photographer Bettina Rheims, in which youngsters are portrayed naked against a neutral background with gender characteristics opposed to their sex. The Belgian artist Marie-Jo Lafontaine can be mentioned as well in this respect. In her photographic work she also takes an interest in the youth portrait. Characteristic of her work is the combining of close ups of children and adolescents with monochrome colour surfaces (like in *Savoir retenir et fixer ce qui est sublime* (1989)) or with text (like in *La vie ... une hésitation* (1992)), which strengthens the meaning of the photographic portrait.

After *Personae* Malou Swinnen continued with black-and-white photography, which for the second time reached the summit in the artist book *Surface* (1999). This publication contains the same basic elements like *Personae* (naked, female models, whether or not provided with an attribute), but is more experimental on a typographic level: the pictures -which often only reveal a fragment of the original image, are lacking uniformity as far as size, and seem to jump randomly on the page.

The application of the portrait genre turns out to be symptomatic of the Belgian avant-gardist photo scene of the 1980s. This is clearly illustrated by the fact that half of the by the gallery 't Pepertje exhibited photography during the art exhibition Linea '83 consisted of portraits, and the magazine *XYZ* integrally dedicated an issue to the Belgian portrait photography in 1984. In my opinion the portrait is in fact a crucial factor in the process of the insertion of photography in the Belgian art scene. Individuals like Dirk Braeckman, Liliane Vertessen and Jan Vercruysse for example managed to think beyond the strict borders of art photography and to use the medium to create works of art. They realized photographic images which should not be grasped within photography, but rather within art. The techniques applied for this purpose are quite different: through a far reaching manipulation in the dark room, Braeckman introduced stains and streaks, tones of grey and a certain blur into his 'spontaneous portraits' of the 1980s, attaching a special pictorial quality to the images. Vertessen adds neon lamps and brightly coloured feathers to her provocative self portraits through which the images do not only work two-dimensionally but also in three dimensions. And Vercruysse in his *Portretten van de Kunstenaar* (a book that was published in 1997 and which contains images of 1977-84) manipulates photography in the form of offset printing or photolithographs, composed and structured in a complex way in order to make conceptual art. A possible explanation for the multiple use of the portrait in the process of the entry of photography in the Belgian art scene could be the tradition of painting which is very manifest in our regions and in which the portrait has played an important role for centuries.

The way in which Malou Swinnen relates to the Belgian photographic scene of the 1980s, has already been mentioned with regard to her debut images. With her first colour pictures she deviates from the pretty dominant black-and-white (portrait-)tradition. Still, her whole oeuvre in which the portrait is being investigated by experimenting with light-dark effects, poses and attributes, does fit the process that we have just sketched. In this process photography in Belgium – by means of the portrait genre among others – tears itself loose from the strict codes of art photography and is accepted little by little as a 'full' artistic medium. Also Swinnen's return to colour photography in 2000 can be grasped in the light of this evolution.

Back to colour

Malou Swinnen: *"After* Surface *(1999), which was a kind of round-up of black-and-white photography during the last 10 years, I wanted to return to colour photography. I wanted to explore the depiction of the skin in colour, after my research of the representation of the sensuality of the skin on a photographic surface in black-and-white photography. I remained loyal to my main theme – the portrait.* Young and Beautiful *consists of portraits of young people as they appear to me, with clothes, hair, make-up which they have chosen themselves. I chose those youngsters who reminded me of pictures of movie stars, pop and rock musicians (James Dean, Sean Penn, Sofia Coppola, Raquel Welch, etc), whom I had seen in magazines, newspapers or on television. In this series I have also decided to direct only little. I simply asked them to take place in front of the camera."*

In *Young and Beautiful* (2001) the photographer thus takes up again the same sources of inspiration (films and music videos) which laid the foundations for her first colour portraits. The protagonists again are contemporary boys and girls. However, compared to the work of the 1980s the setting and atmosphere are less cinematographic, less glamorous, less artificial. Leaving out pieces of scenery and forced poses generates a certain neutrality which reminds us of the portraits of Thomas Ruff, photographed in the 1980s. With Ruff, Swinnen shares the interest in depicting the individual in a contemporary manner. *Young and Beautiful* offers a sampling of the appearance of young people anno 2001. The use of the bust portrait against a monochrome background results in the creation of an extreme proximity and impenetrable closeness at the same time. No matter how closely or how long we can watch the figure, his or her identity will never be completely revealed.

The same idea of 'elusiveness' is also translated into *De Pose* (2002). This series of nude portraits which can be divided into smaller sequences of two to five images per model, shows an intimacy as well as a cold aloofness. By showing 2, 3, 4 or 5 poses per person (cut off at knee height) Swinnen starts adding up until 100, 1000, 10000,... The identity cannot or can never be grasped. Once again the focus in these works is on the skin: a young, healthy skin with small imperfections generating a vulnerability and beauty. Still, this is not what attracts the observer's attention. Sliding across the photographic surface his gaze is drawn to the face. The face (with the eyes as 'spearheads') forms a kind of magnetic core which imprisons the observer and forces him to introspection.

Between *Young and Beautiful* and *De Pose* Malou Swinnen regularly abandoned the serenity of the photo studio to throw herself into the radically different atmosphere of the dazzling nightlife. For two years she has been frequenting the club LAROCCA in Lier whose motto 'famous and original' she gloriously illustrates.

Malou Swinnen: *"My interest in glamour and the dream world made me go to the discotheque. There is plenty of posing going on there. The people going out in the discotheque can only communicate by their clothes, hair, make-up, attributes, tattoos. It is the place to see and to be seen. People can barely talk to each other because the music is very loud. Everything is done by their looks. Everything is surface. My photographs became an ode to nightlife. Here for the first time I carried a small handheld camera while mingling with other people on the dance floor taking pictures of them in an informal reportage style. Yet I never did so without asking for their permission with my eyes. I combined these pictures with photographs taken with my Hasselblad camera which I had set up in my mobile studio next to the dance floor. I asked beautiful people to pose for me."*

Again, and now even stronger, the colourful images of Nan Goldin come to mind. But - just like Swinnen indicates herself - she only concentrates on the outward appearance, while Goldin - because of her personal relationship with the 'models' - also 'portrays' exemplae of friendship, love, emotion, sadness, happiness… Swinnen shows the temptation, the fun, the ecstasy which only takes place between the walls of the discotheque.

Finally, from the whirling on the dance floor to the calm atmosphere of the museum in *Cet obscur objet…* (2005). Commissioned by the Stedelijk Museum Vander Kelen-Mertens in Leuven, Malou Swinnen carefully picked out some objects of the collection (a book, a fan, a key, a mantel clock, etc.) which she photographed in combination with dark-skinned models. Combining the nude with an attribute, as seen in *Personae* and *Surface*, seems to resurrect again as a successful formula.

Malou Swinnen: *"This time it is about the representation of the sensuality of the dark skin in colour. I ask the naked models to close their eyes so all the attention is drawn to the object. I aimed to show another view of the objects from a Western museum, represented on the dark skin of people of African origin."*

1985-2005

From *Faces & Fascinations* (1985) to *Cet obscur objet…* (2005) Malou Swinnen follows a headstrong course in which she mixes conventional elements with personal interests. Starting in a period in which the 'institutional' context at first sight was not unfavourable for a starting photographer, she bravely made her debut with portraits in colour. Thus, she should be less associated with the Belgian artistic context, but rather with the more international phenomenon of the 'pictures'.

A strong interest in the 'essence of photography' leads her to black-and-white photography where she profoundly studies the traditional portrait genre and translates it into a very personal iconography. The core of her photographic research – the representation of the skin and the face – finally brings her back to colour photography which she is exploring more and more - also in the present book.

1 For example in the Ecole Nationale Supérieure des Arts Visuels in La Cambre, the institute 75 in Brussels, the Académie des Beaux-Arts in Charleroi, the Institut des Beaux-Arts in Liège, the College St. Lukas Brussels, the Koninklijke Academie voor Schone Kunsten in Ghent, and thus also the Stedelijke Academie voor Schone Kunsten in Hasselt.

2 This assumption has recently been confirmed during a debate, titled 'De relatie Vlaanderen-Wallonië, onbekender dan het buitenland?' at the symposium *Belgian Art Reconsidered* in the Castle of Boechout, National Botanical Garden of Belgium, Meise, on the 12th of May 2006 organized by the Lieven Gevaert Centre.

3 Phototechnically Swinnen realizes the depiction of the skin by means of a focus on the 'zone 6'. In the academy it was Ernest Franssens who taught her about this zone system and who learned it from Ansel Adams in the U.S.A.

Bibliography

ANDRIES, Pool, 'Mise-en-Scène. De Realiteit van de Verbeelding', in : *Mise-en-Scène. De Realiteit van de Verbeelding*, exhib. cat., Antwerp: Museum voor Fotografie, 1988: n.p.

CRIMP, Douglas, 'Pictures', *October*, 8, 1979: pp. 75-88.

D'HOOGHE, Alain, 'Verzonnen beelden en fragmenten van de realiteit. Enkele aspecten van de fotografie sinds de jaren 1980', in: Georges Vercheval (ed.), *Pour une Histoire de la Photographie en Belgique. Essais critiques – Répertoire des photographes depuis 1839,* Charleroi: Musée de la Photographie, 1993: pp.312-316.

SALU, Luc, 'De fotografische tijdschriften', in: Georges Vercheval (ed.), *Pour une Histoire de la Photographie en Belgique. Essais critiques – Répertoire des photographes depuis 1839*, Charleroi: Musée de la Photographie, 1993: pp. 267-271.

SARLET, Jean-Michel, 'Van de jaren '50 naar de jaren '70. Van het individuele naar het collectieve, van de marginaliteit naar een relatieve rechtmatigheid', in: Georges Vercheval (ed.), *Pour une Histoire de la Photographie en Belgique. Essais critiques – Répertoire des photographes depuis 1839*, Charleroi: Musée de la Photographie, 1993: pp. 305-310.

VAN GELDER, Hilde, *De plaats en betekenis van de fotografie als medium binnen de artistieke context van de late jaren '50 tot nu. Een bespreking aan de hand van kunstkritische teksten*, MA thesis, Katholieke Universiteit Leuven, 1995.

WEINBERG, Jonathan, 'Fantastic Tales. The Photography of Nan Goldin', in: *Fantastic Tales. The Photography of Nan Goldin,* London: Tate Publishing, 2005: pp. 1-30.

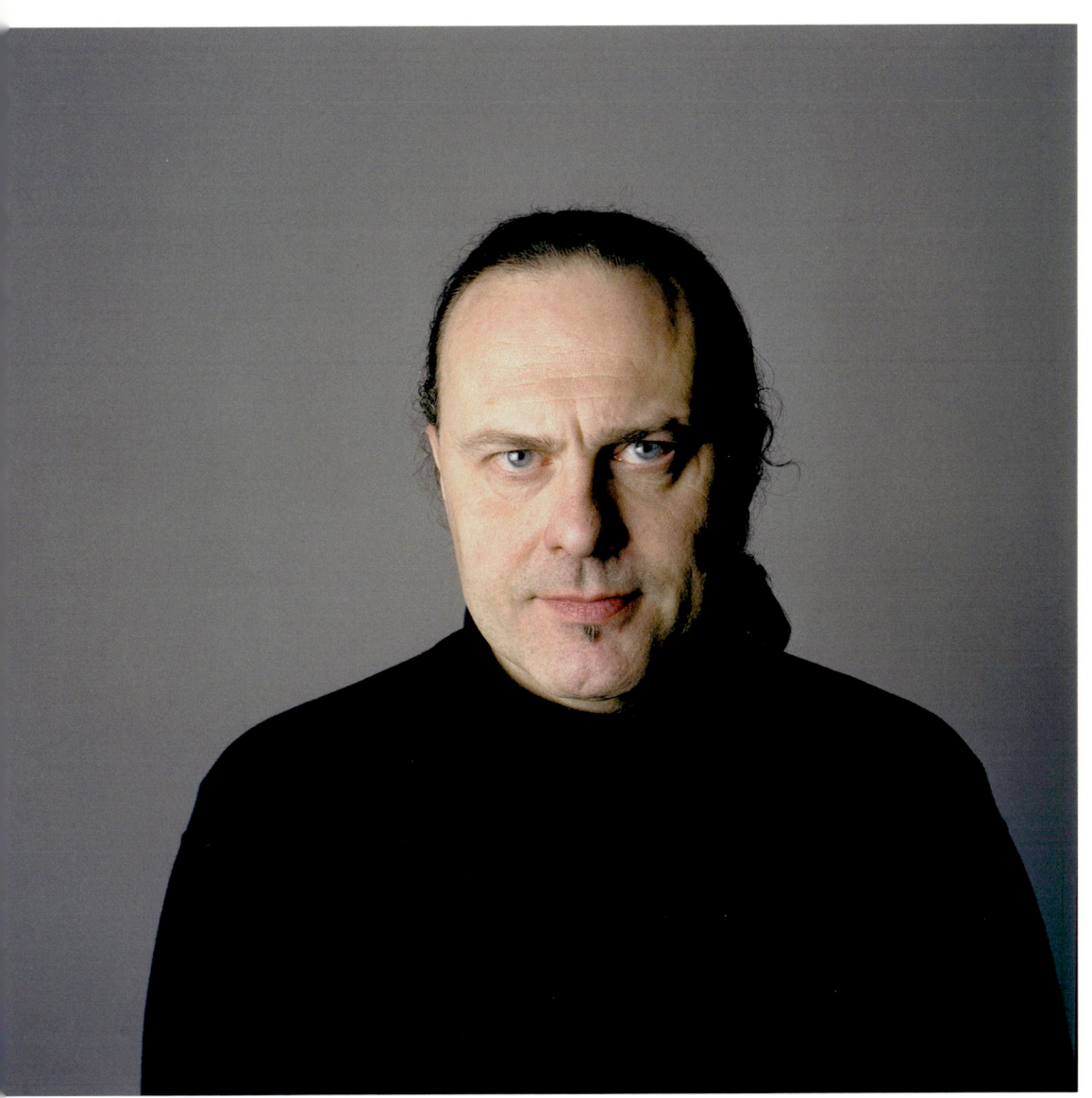

1. Eric Sleichim

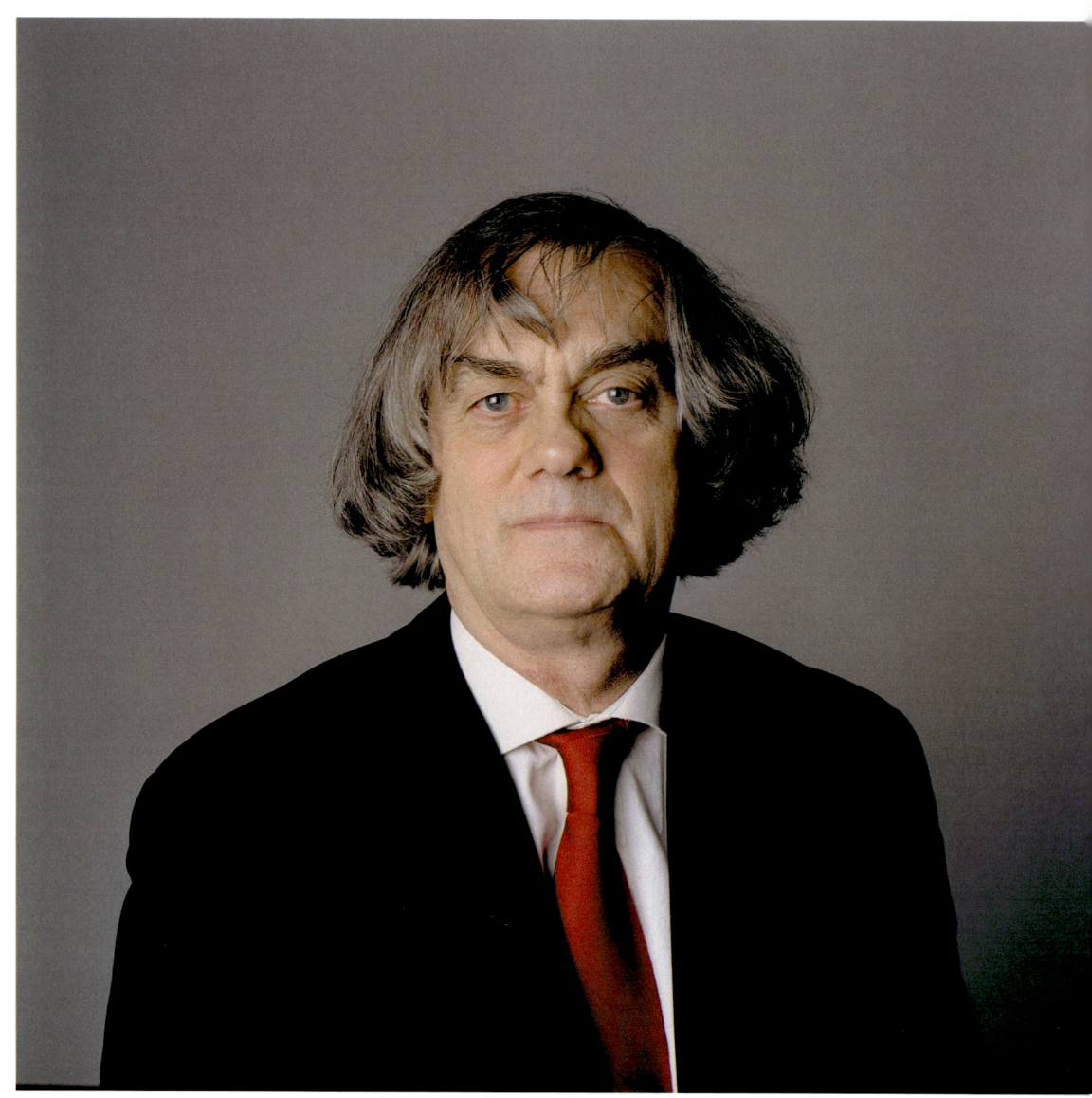

2. Sigiswald Kuijken

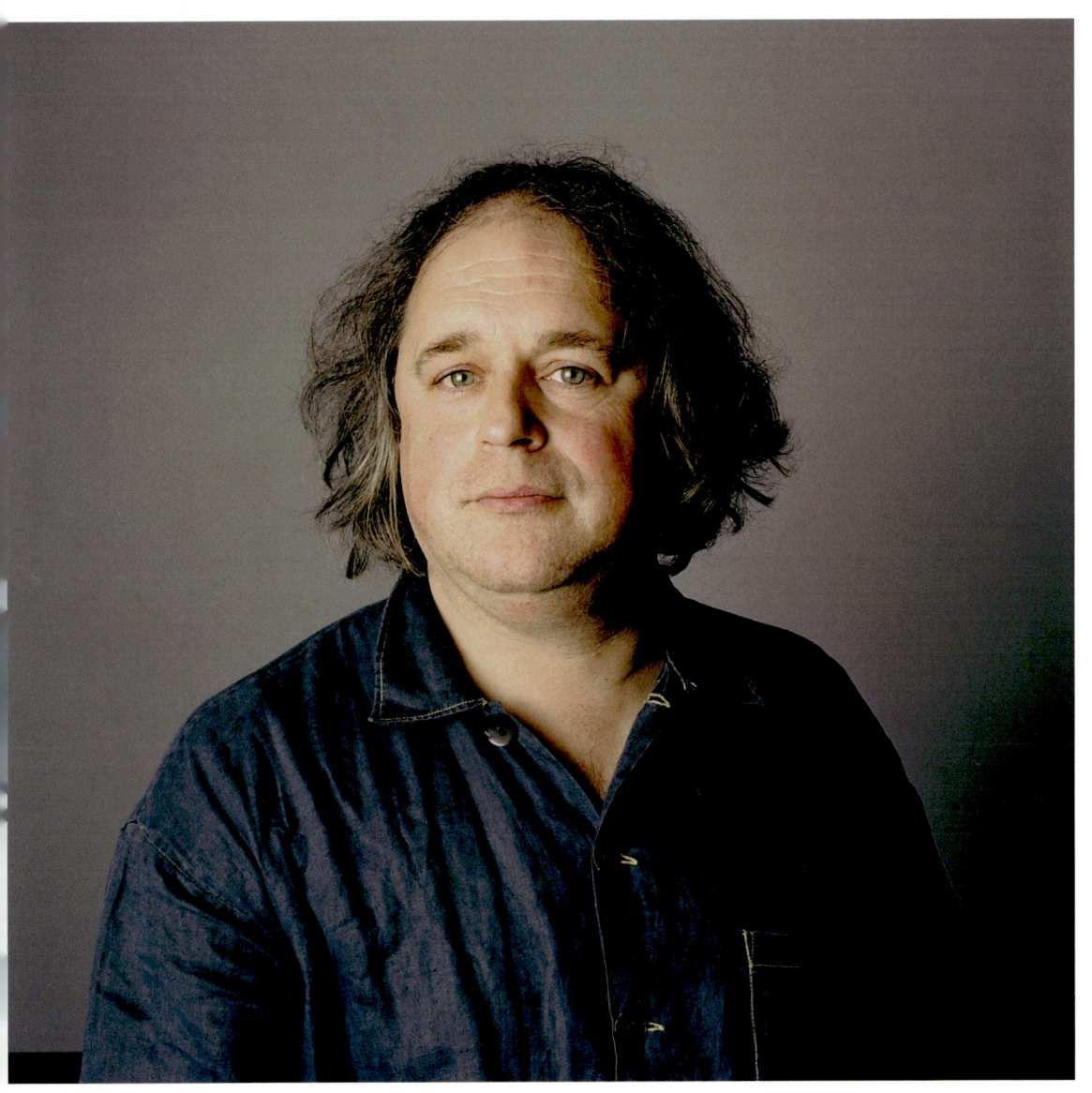

3. Marcel Ponseele

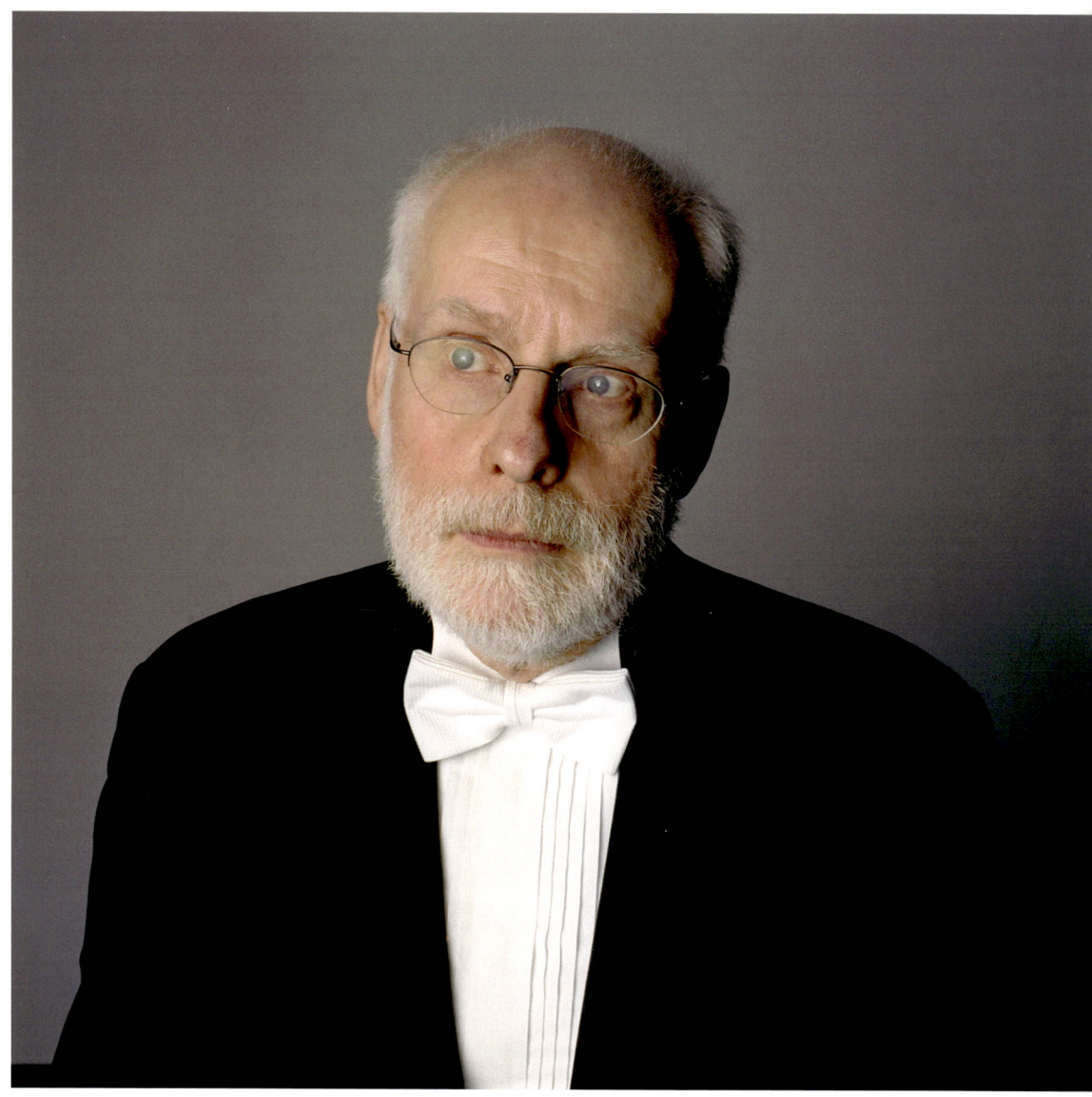

4. Ton Koopman

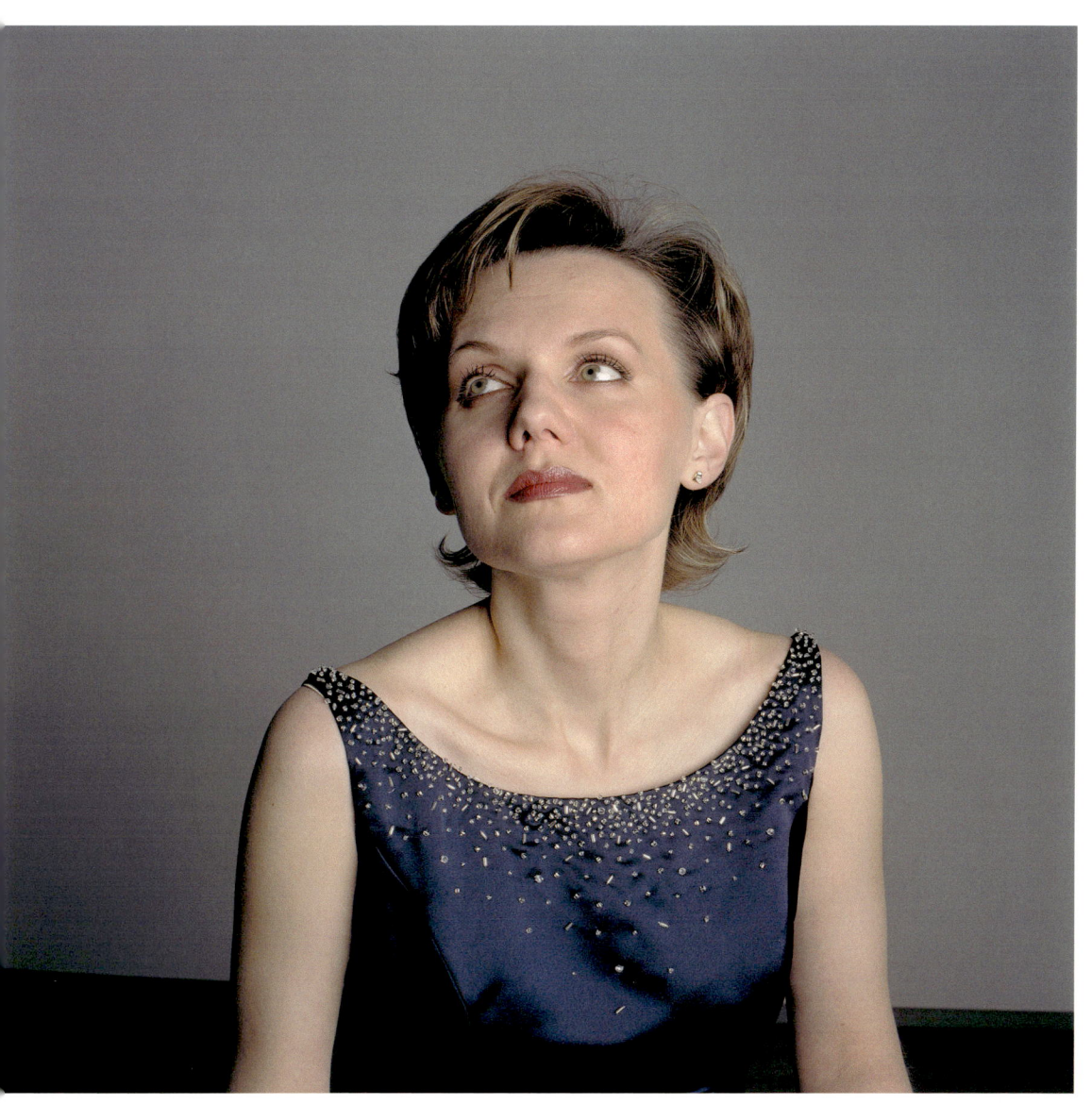

5. Olga Pasichnyk

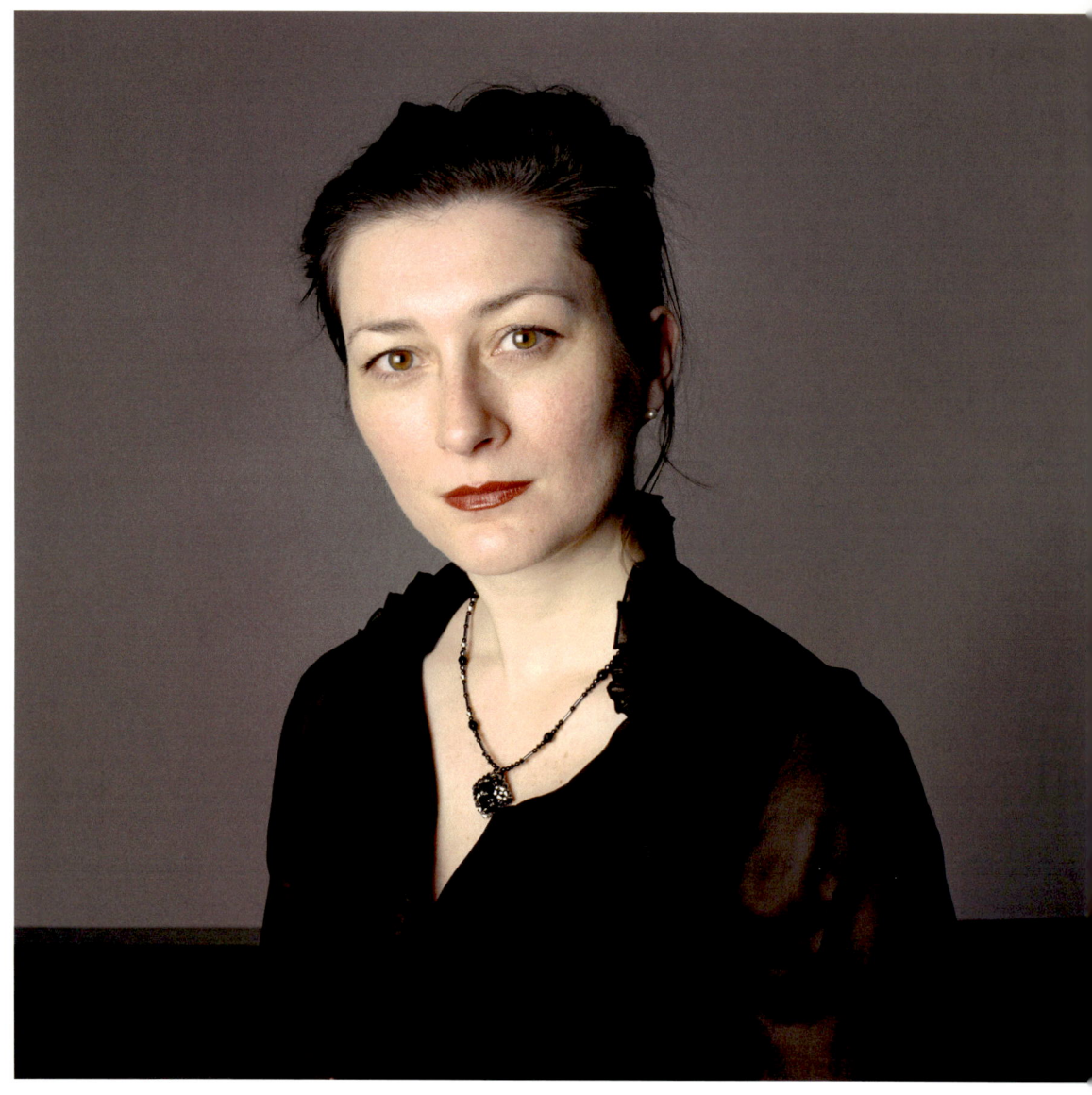

6. Claire Chevallier

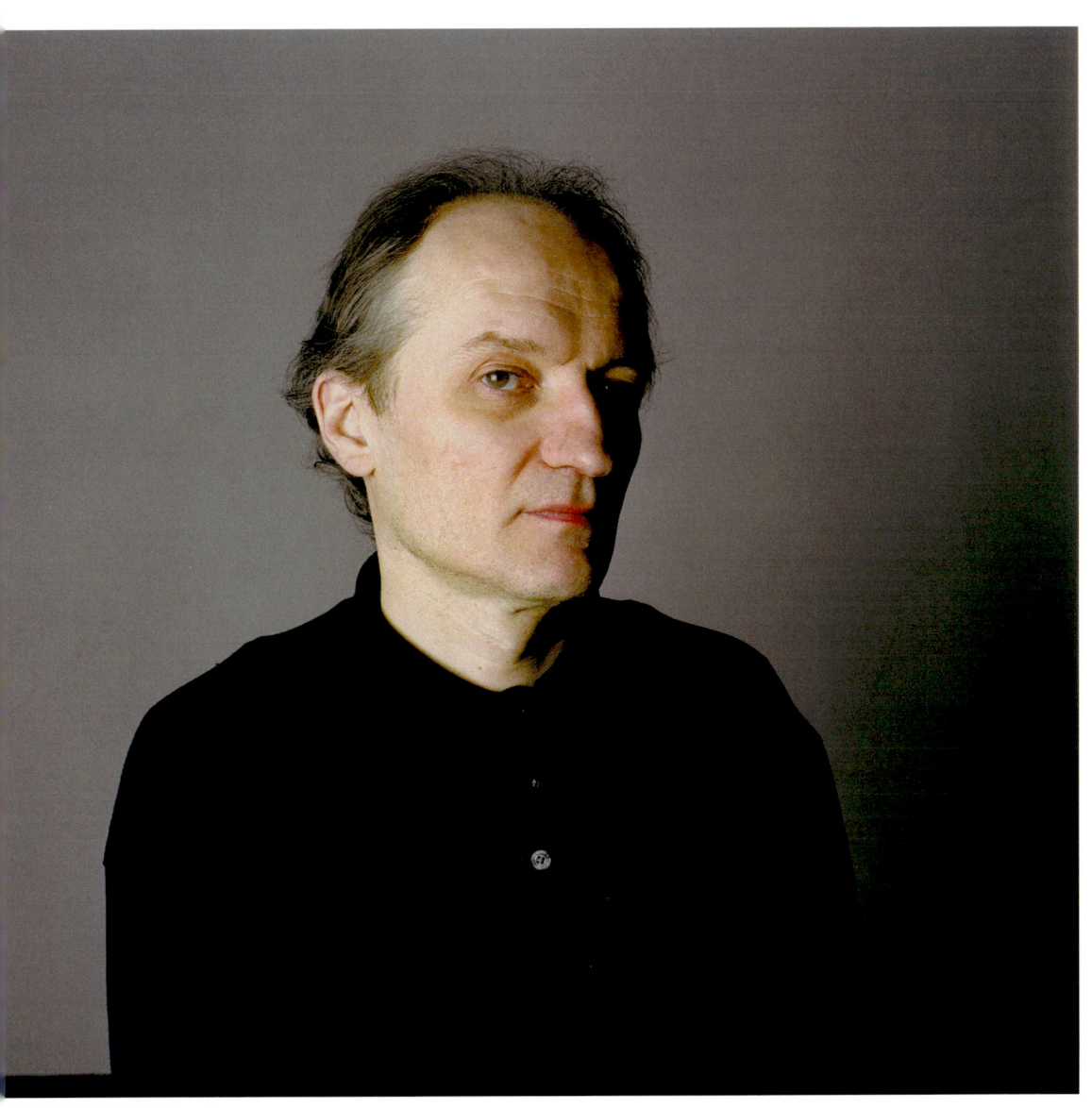

7. Erik Vermeulen

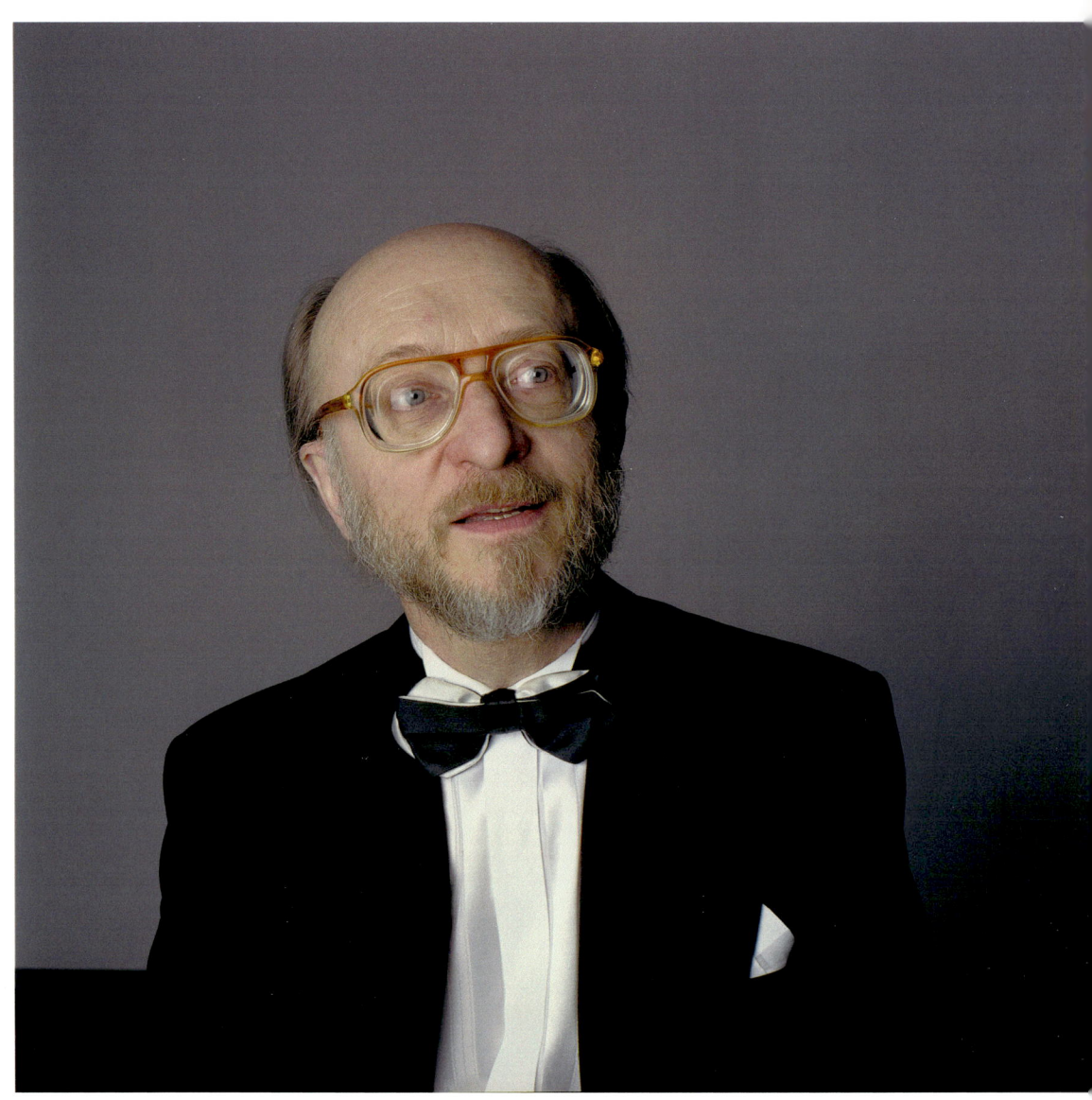

8. Alexei Lubimov

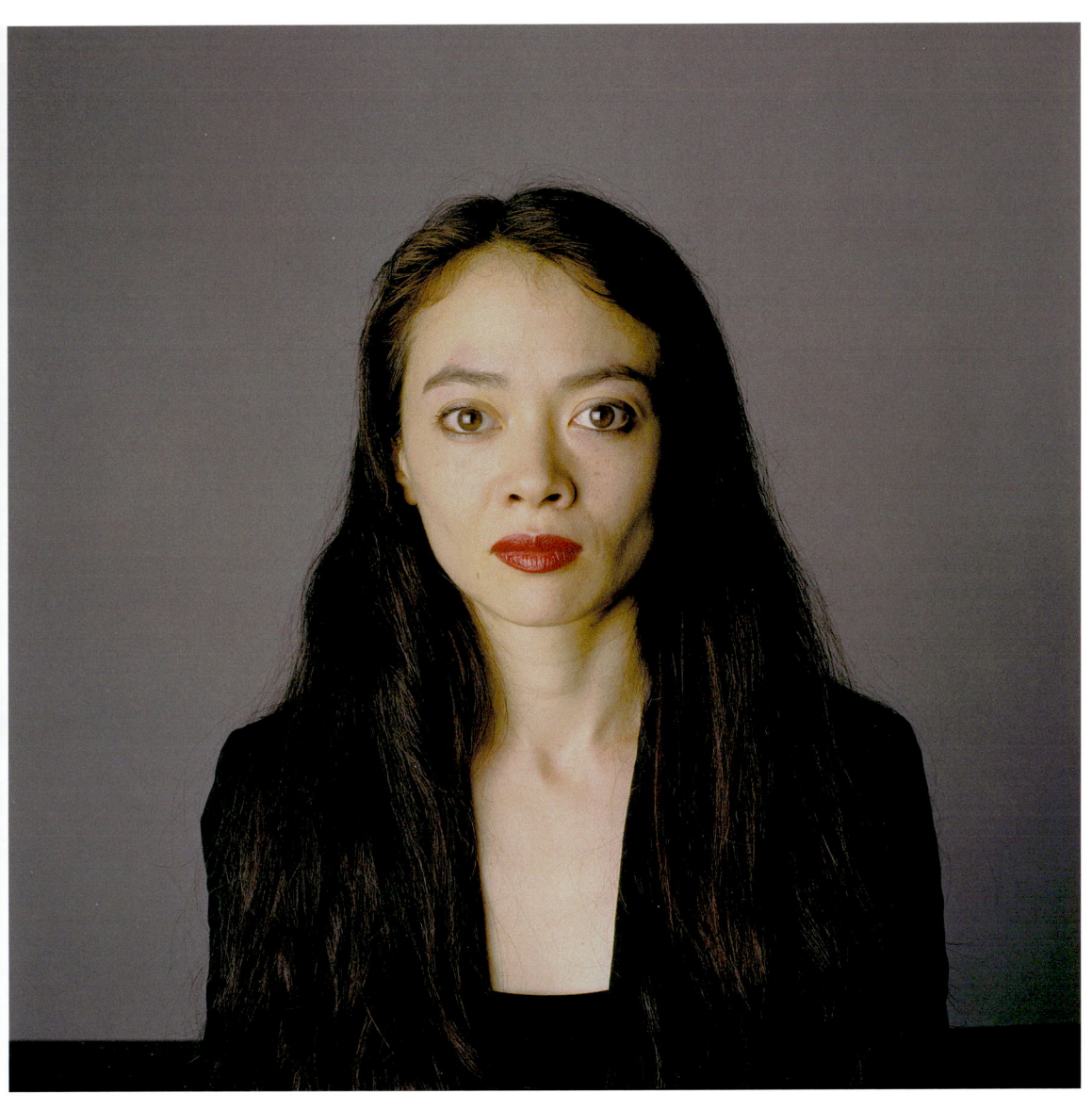

9. Midori Seiler

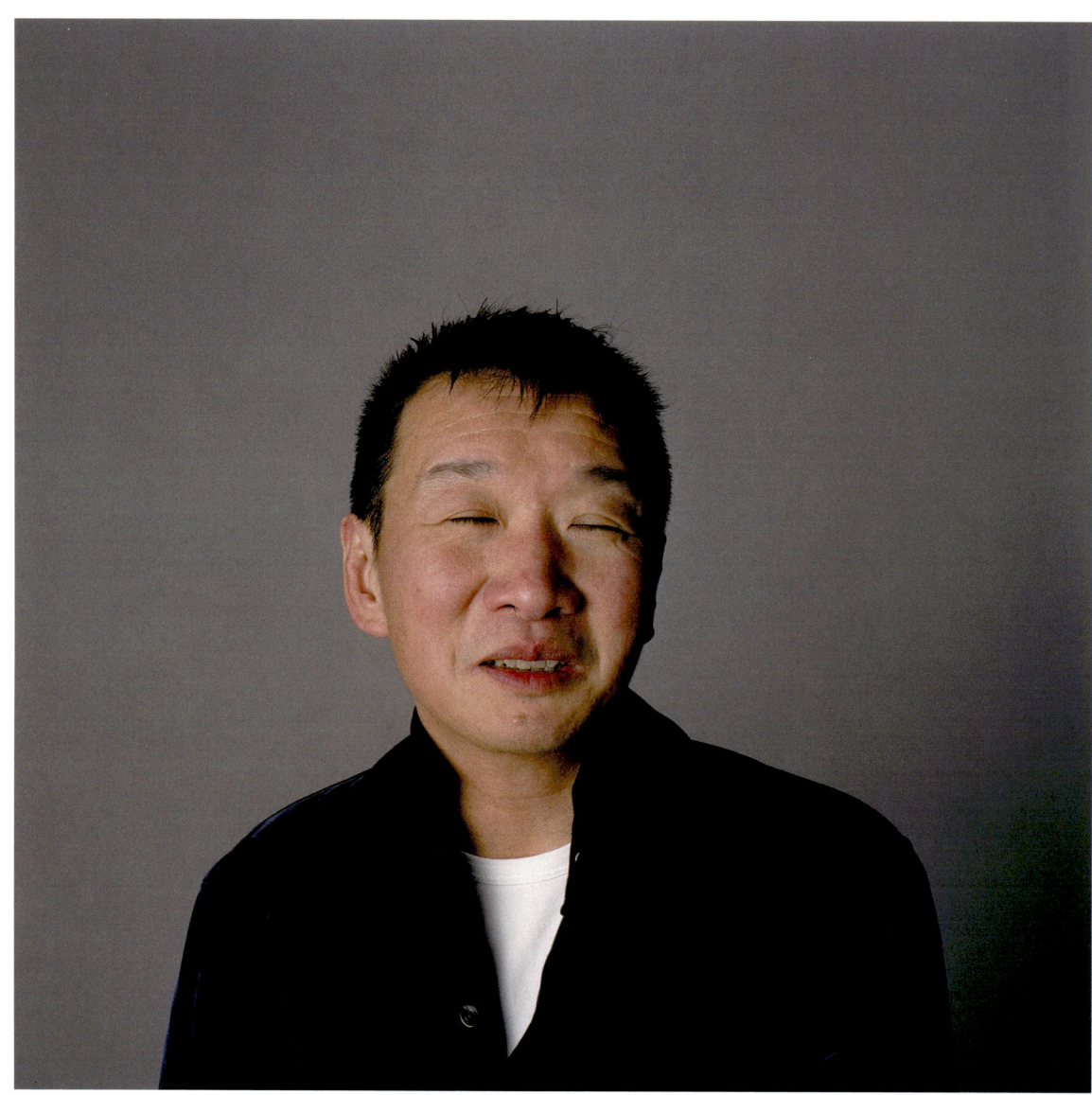

10. Melvyn Tan

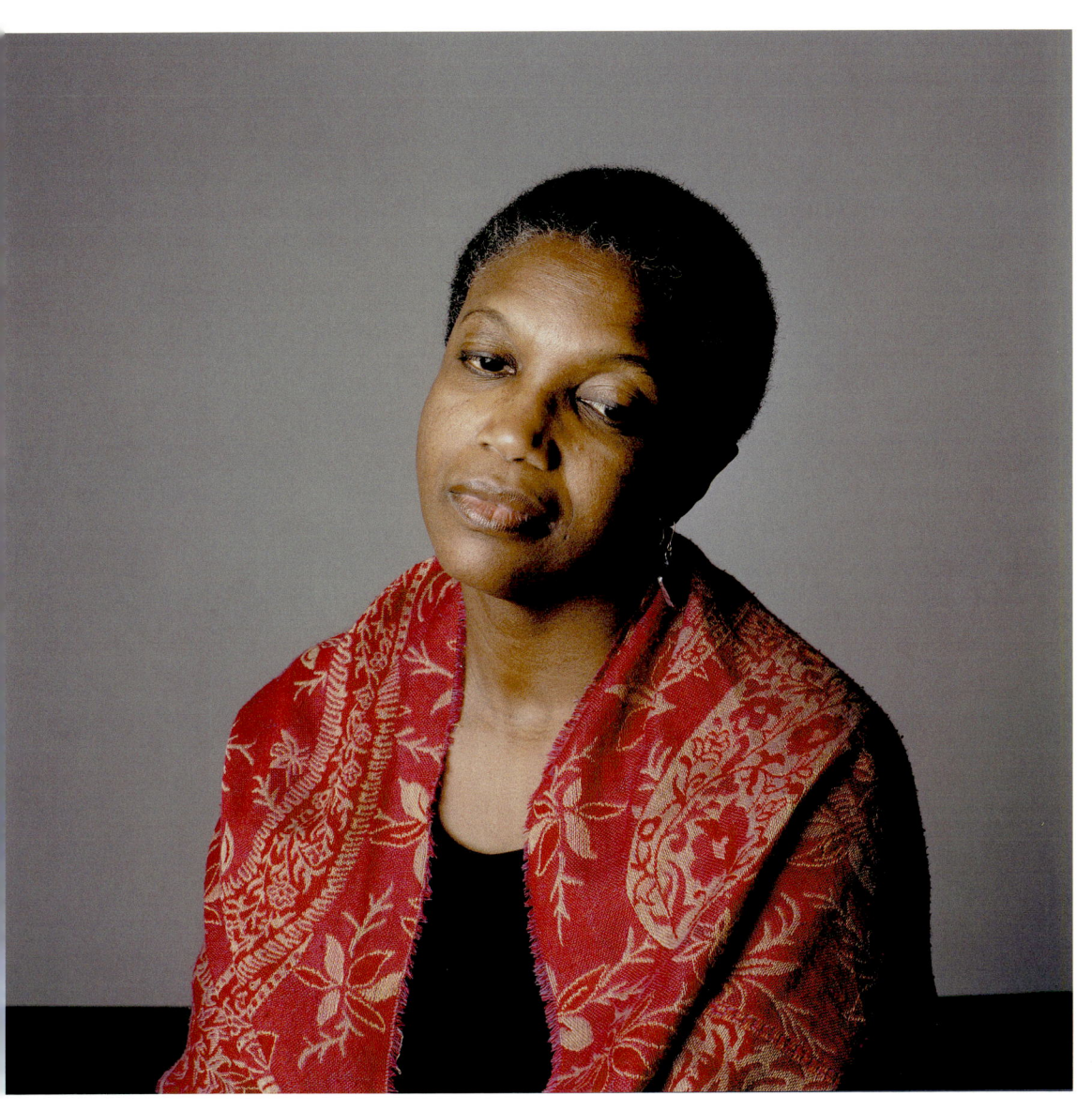

11. Claron McFadden

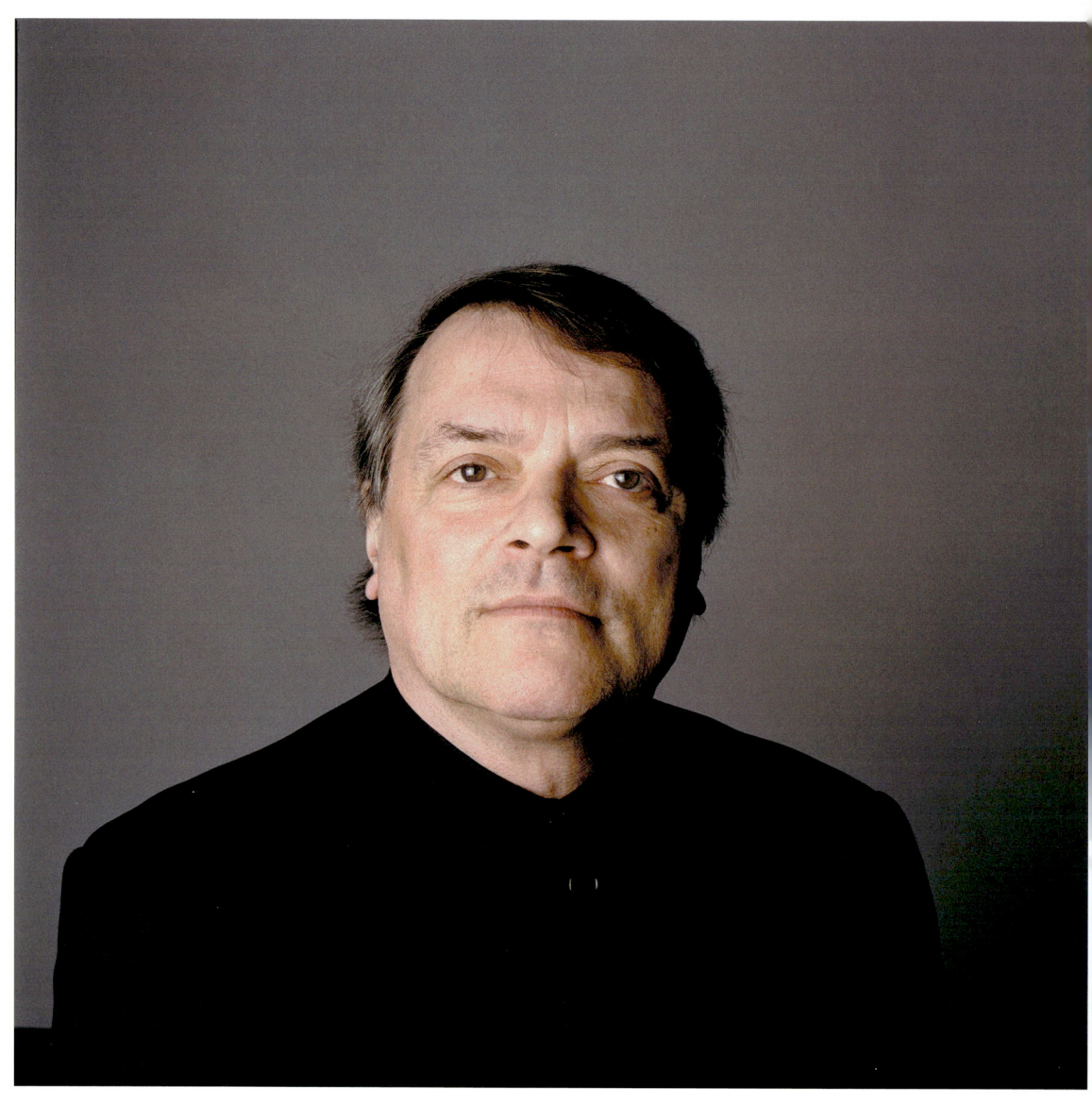

12. Jos van Immerseel

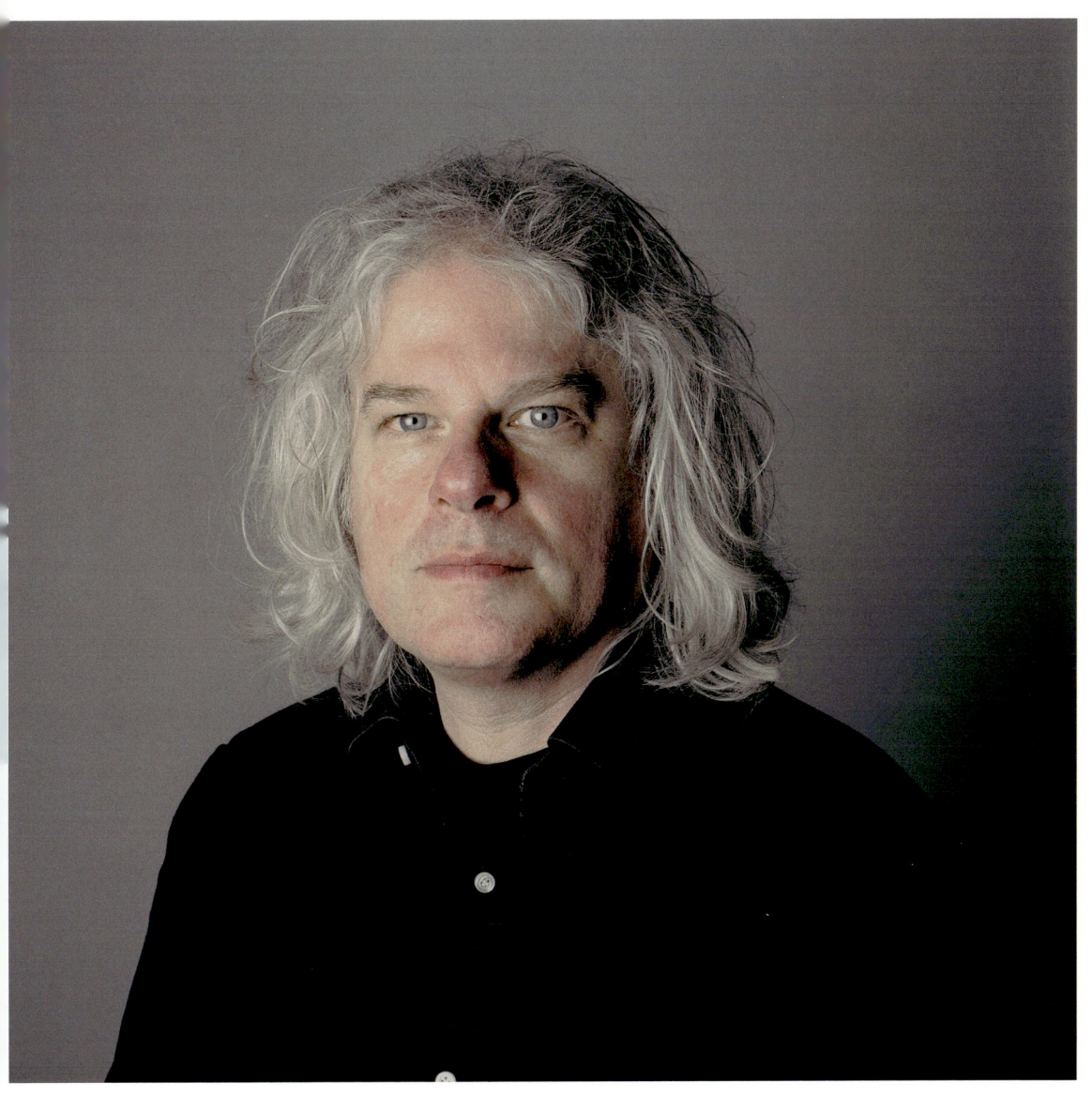

13. Ronald Brautigam

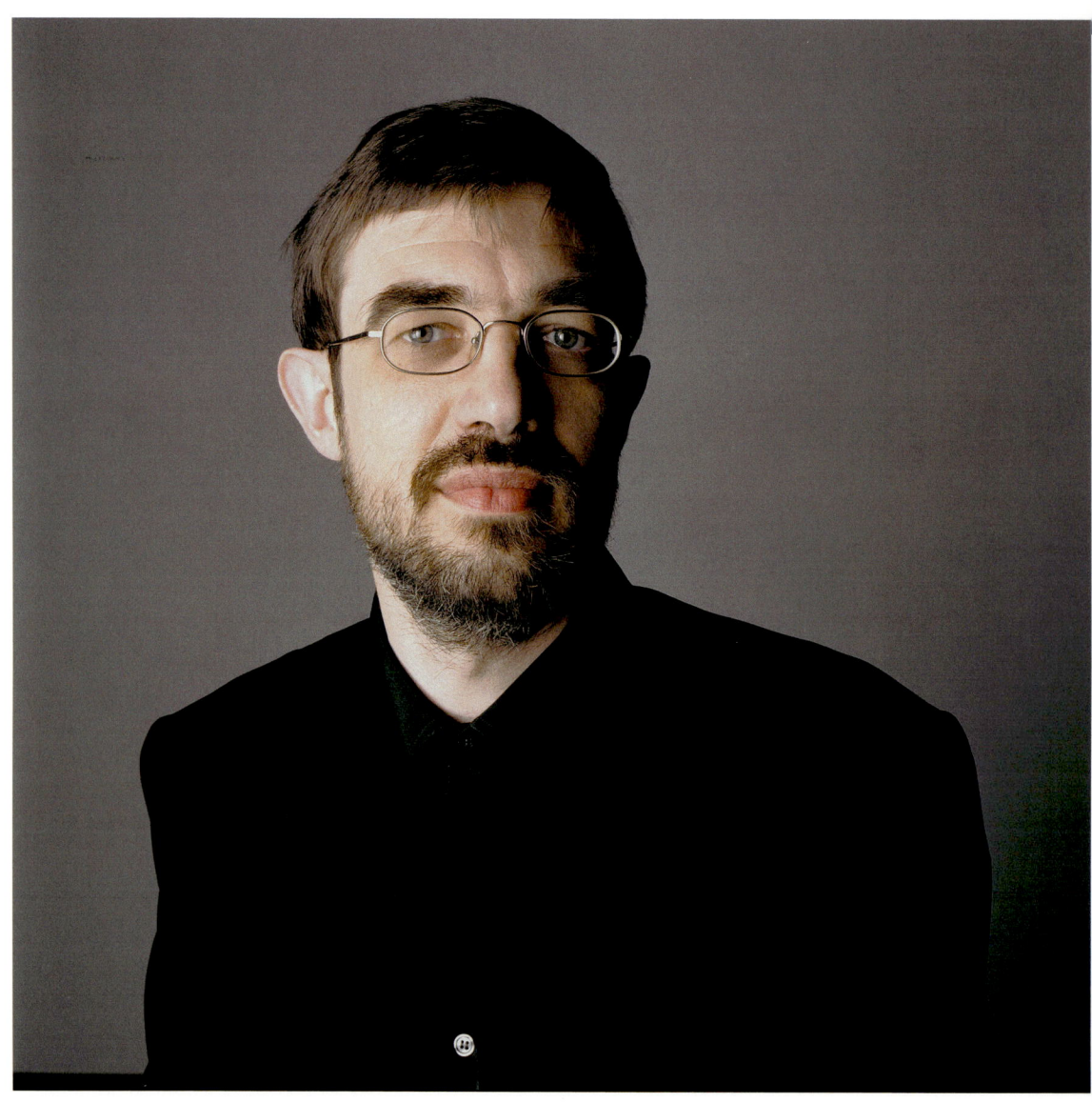

14. Jan Michiels

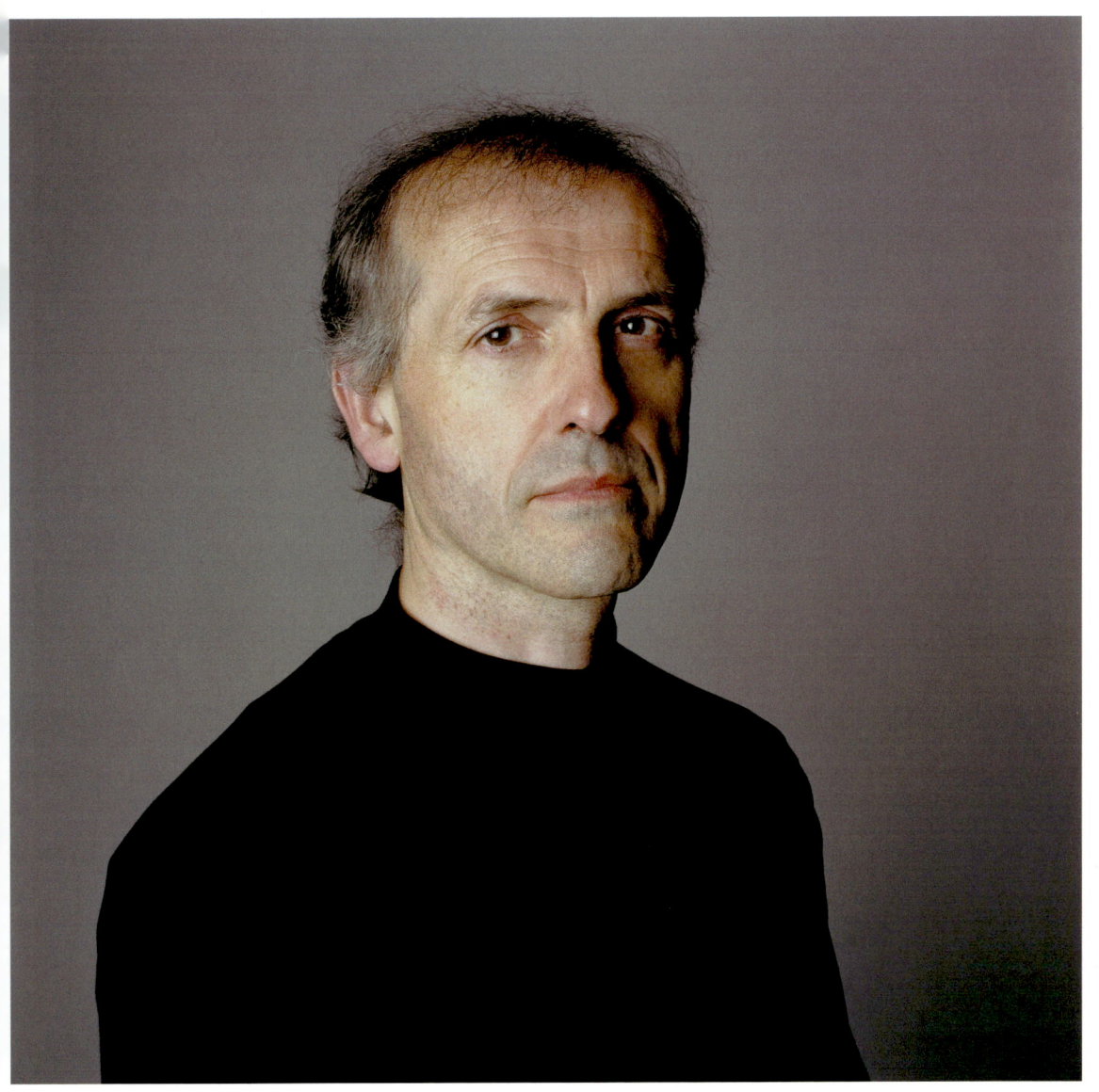

15. Roel Dieltiens

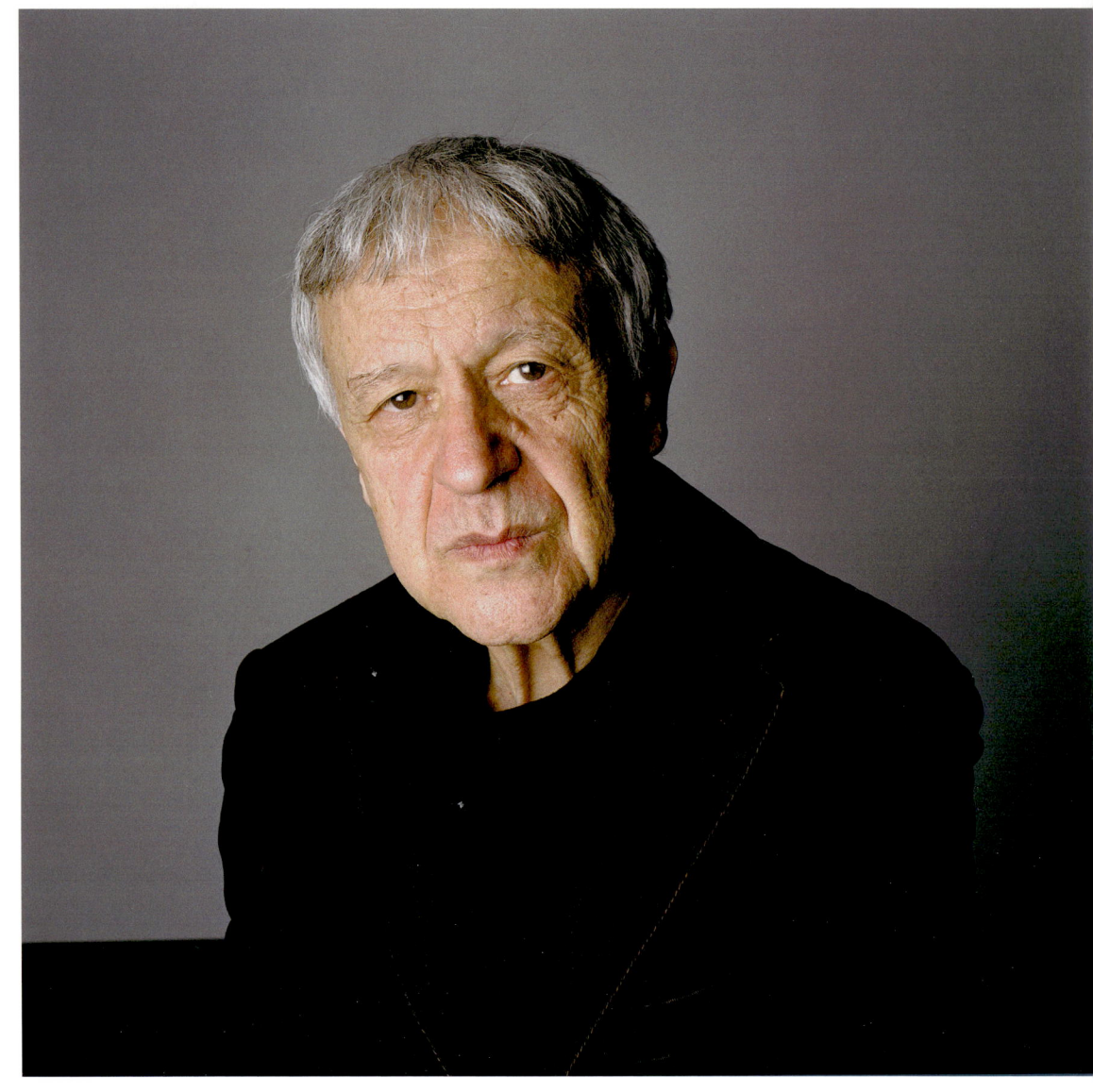

16. Michel Portal

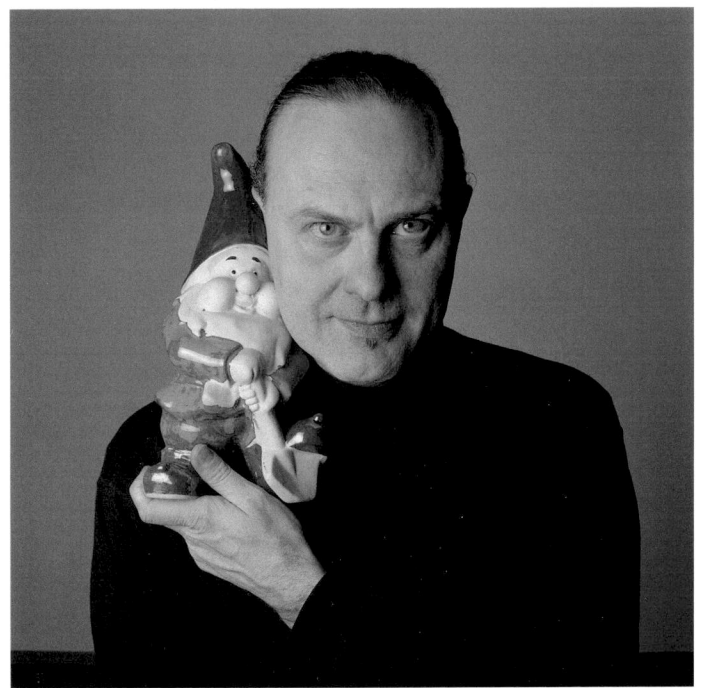

Sans paroles

Eric Sleichim

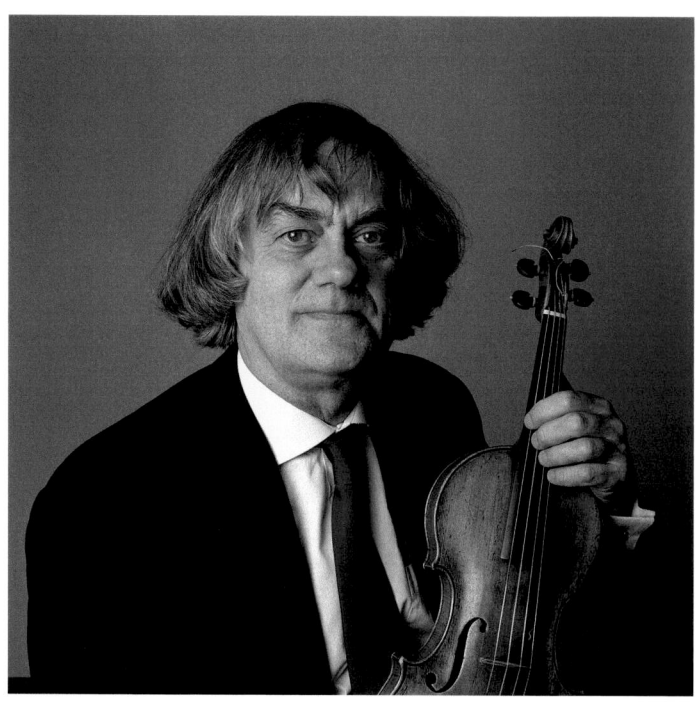

Every human being is unique, this we already know by now. In each one of us a life core is hiding that we can barely reach ourselves (let alone others...) – covered by a haze, a veil draped over the sparkling inner point, darkening and concealing its shine from ourselves and our congeners. Mysticians from all times and cultures call this inner point by many names, and – it keeps stammering.

Between Mozart and us, it almost seems as if this cloak does not exist, this is how close his mystery is to ours. Sometimes he is referred to as the "divine" Mozart – and I am starting to think that maybe that expression is not as ordinary as it seems at first sight: out of his music the unspeakable speaks, the unfathomable sounds, the silence trembles, tears laugh and laughs weep...

The point we cannot reach: listen quietly to Mozart, you're (almost) there!

Sigiswald Kuijken

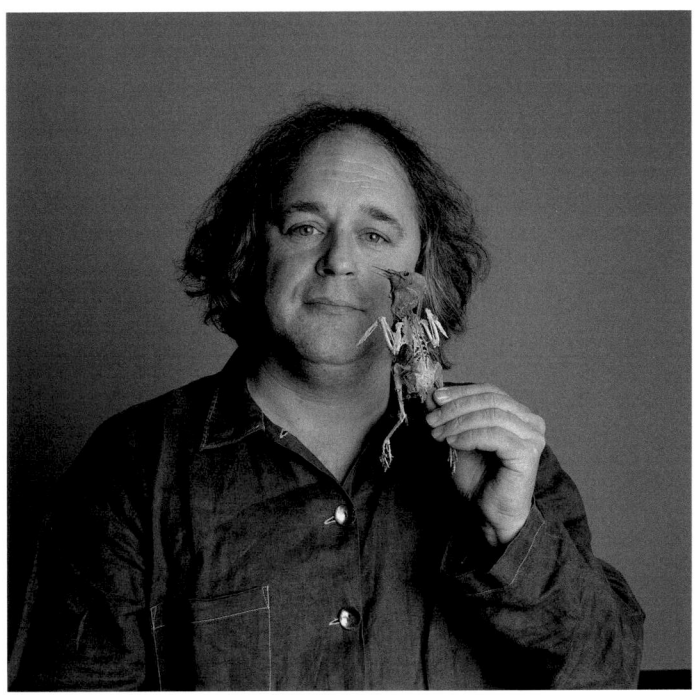

Mozart's father, Leopold, died on 28 May 1787 at the age of 68. The man who had dedicated himself to his children's careers during his whole life, was buried in Salzburg. However, the main absentee during his burial service was his son Wolfgang… due to illness. Not a week after his father's death, Wolfgang's pet died as well…a sparrow! Mozart writes an amusing epitaph in honour of the deceived bird (http://www.starlingtalk.com/mozart3.htm#poem).

The thing that always fascinated me about Mozart, is the contrast between the genius in and of his music on the one hand and his childlike reactions on the other. From a very young age he already showed a very mature musical development, yet his letters show a rather 'crude' Mozart or 'fäkalko-mischer Art', to put it in the German Mozart biographers' words. How can someone whose father just died write a light-hearted poem about the death of his sparrow? Wouldn't this rather have been a reaction to his education?

No doubt father Leopold only wanted the best for his son when travelling with his children through-out Europe, hoping to offer them the best possible future. He did not want them to be tied to one royal court or another as a lackey/musician where they would be allowed to make some music once in a while after taking care of the castle. From his childhood on, Mozart had always been treated as an adult. For instance, he used to wear adult clothing, children's size indeed. Too many times he had to wait for some king to receive him, he had to respect the court's etiquette, memorise all sorts of polite phrases, act humble, travel all the time, sleep at inns…He was this little boy trapped in a world of grown-ups! Our Wolfgang never had the chance to be a child…Wouldn't this deeply affect a person?

A great deal of the energy one normally needs when growing up and becoming an adult had already been used for other goals; that fuel had almost solely been spent on music. Of course one will have to pay for this in the end… On the 6th of December 1791, the frail and worn out body was descended in a poor man's grave. Mozart…and the bird (sparrow?) had flown, yet his music goes beyond death.

Marcel Ponseele

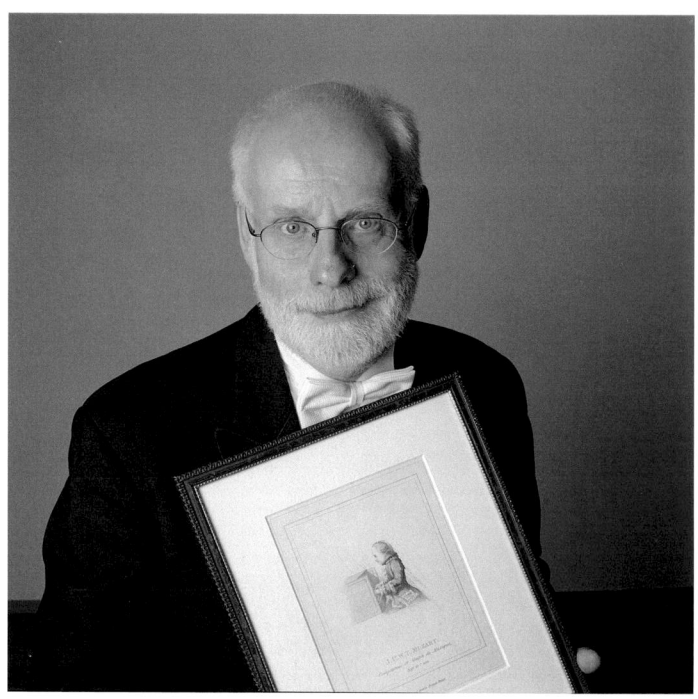

W.A. Mozart went from unique infant prodigy to enfant terrible, and then grew into a complete genius. In spite of their musical achievements, he and his sister Nannerl were never exploited by their father. He saw what they were capable of and during their long journeys he would bring them into contact with many older colleagues. He also let them look at art and gave them an education. Father Mozart was a real "networker".

He had the proper medicines for their regular illnesses. He took care of them, as any father would do. Wolfgang was communicative, though sharp-tongued. However, he was always right when criticizing the work of his colleagues. He knew all too well how it should be done and how it could be done.

To me, the operas and piano concertos (and of course the late symphonies) was what really made him a unique and original composer. If only he had given his amply earned money directly to his dear Constanza, who – in music science - is depicted as a luxury craving doll all too often and very unjustly, he would not have had to experience such a financial disaster. And if it weren't for the bleeding, we would surely have known a whole different Mozart – for he only reached the age of between 35 – who would have been a constant and tough competitor for Beethoven.

Ton Koopman

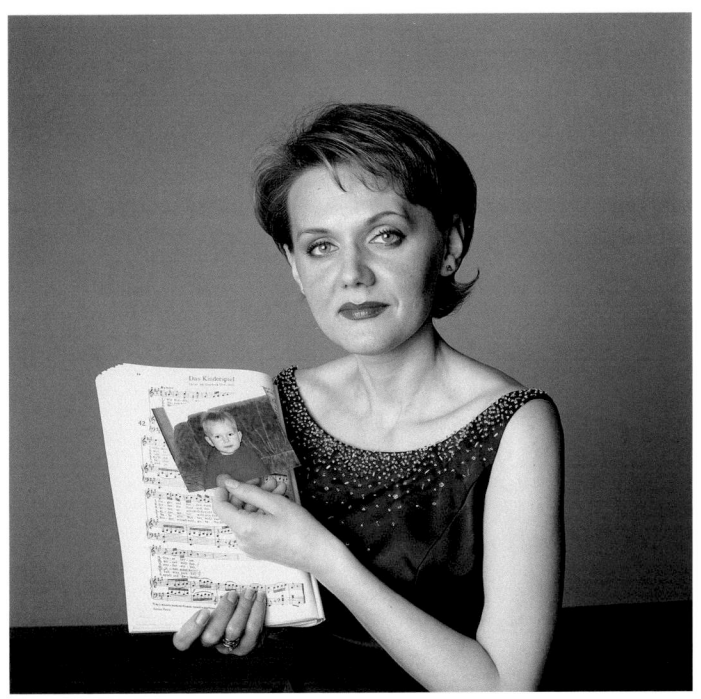

Mozart's music world is like an island, so beautiful and so close,
that apparently you can touch it by hand; you only need two steps to reach it.
I do those two steps, but the distance is still the same…

His music is like the child's game in the sand - easy, open and perfect.
Though to play that game, you have to become a child yourself
- pure, without falseness, authentic discovering the world around for the first time.

I watch my son, listen to Mozart and learn…

Olga Pasichnyk

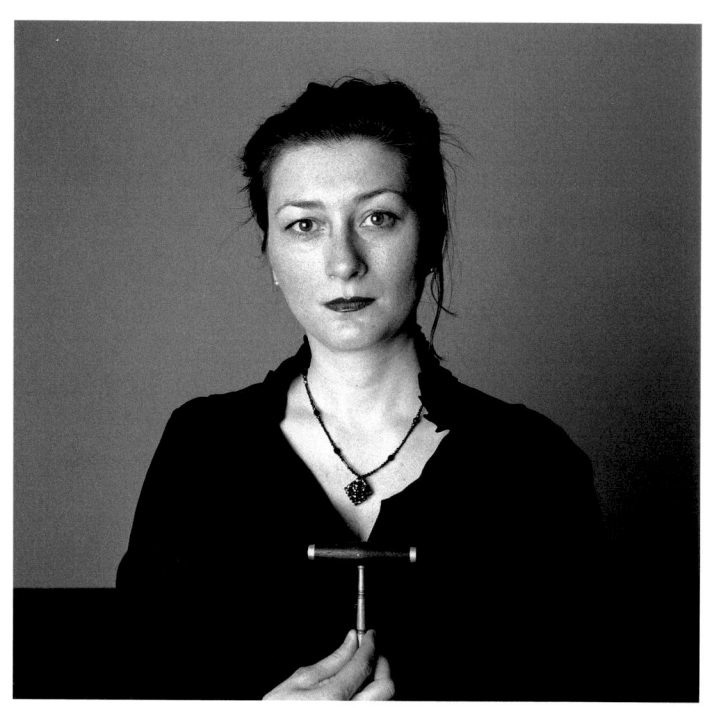

Innocence…drama
Youth…tragedy
Chromatics… spontaneous theatricality
Strict shapes… humour
Intrinsic…Mozart

Claire Chevallier

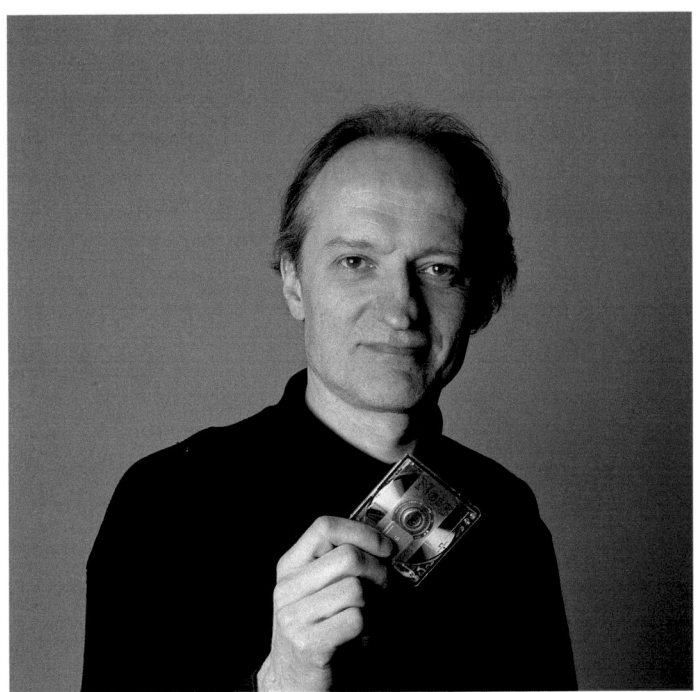

Mozart was part of the soundtrack of my youth.
Since classical music was always on, we often heard Mozart on the radio.
Was it my lack of refinement or musicological-historical insight, or was it the sometimes hopelessly wrong executions which prevented Mozart from making it into my top 5 in those days? Maybe I put his music in one category together with the "table music" of his contemporaries who probably meant well. I don't exactly remember how it was anymore.

Anyway, I'm older and much wiser now. I'm a fan!
Although some nights, certain radio stations, some executions…
In my boldest dreams I take revenge. I present Amadeus the true versions A, B, C ánd D of one of his pieces for him to evaluate, and I exult in his uncensored reaction. Through that very same sound recording medium and a time machine he returns his execution to me with a couple of improvisations and variations on top of it.

Erik Vermeulen

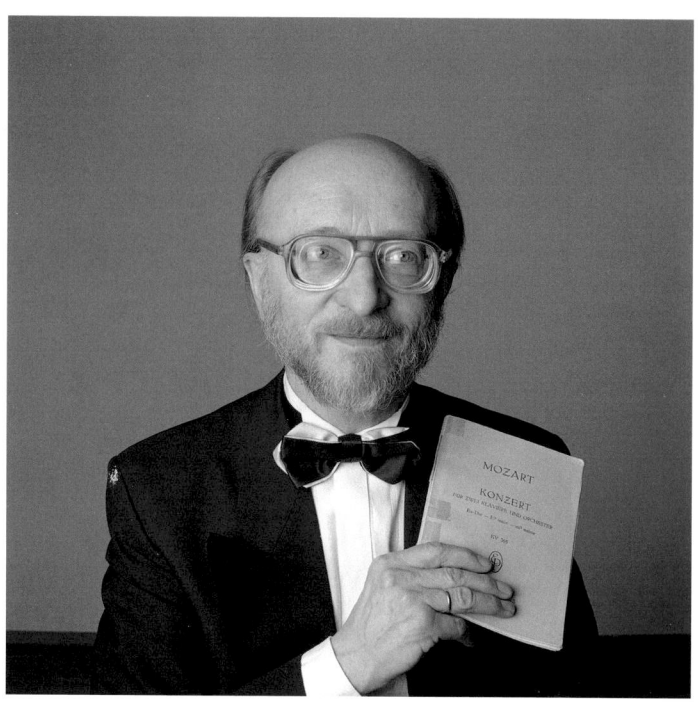

In my youth I was taught to play Mozart in the right style: to produce an exact rendering of the scores, get the phrasing right, and achieve a harmonious balance between tempo and dynamics.

Then, suddenly, at the age of 22, I finally came to understand this: the stylistically appropriate, good looking clothes are only limitations, behind which (at least in my opinion) one main characteristic of Mozart can be detected. A highly changeable, sensitive life, which springs from his music like the varying colours of a chameleon. This is, according to me, the essence of Mozart.

I have become infected by and subject to this sensibility, which covers and reflects all aspects of life: love, death, sorrow, tenderness, fear, passion. It makes me feel like a co-operator of Mozart. He presents himself as a story teller, a director of his own personal theatre, a familiar, friendly companion.

The knowledge of bringing his music to life probably is the most difficult, but also the most valuable for a musician. It is immensely beautiful to be able to learn from Mozart. I will remain one of his students for my whole life.

Alexei Lubimov

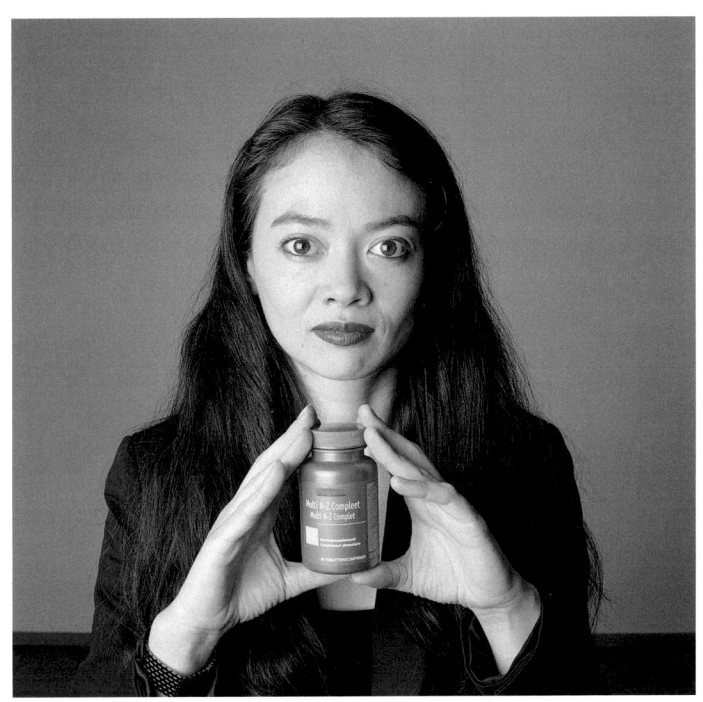

Mozart's music exists in a magnetic field.
It vibrates with its inherent juxtapositions
of the holy and the obscene, of silence and rage,
of bright light-heartedness and the darkest hell.

The cosmos of his music is so complete
that it makes me believe in art's ability to feel
the act of divine creation with the means of a human being.

Midori Seiler

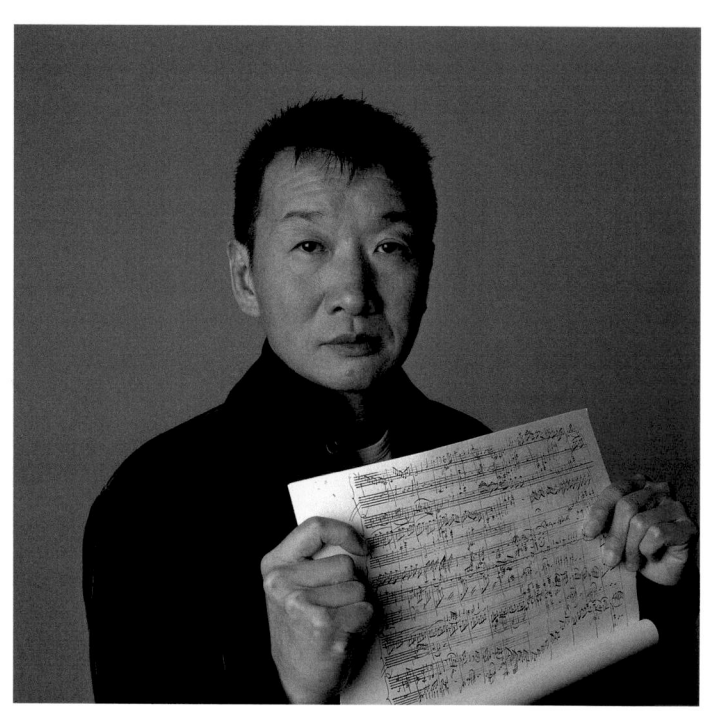

Often the simplest things are the most beautiful and moving,
but always the most difficult.
Such can be said of much of Mozart's music.

Melvyn Tan

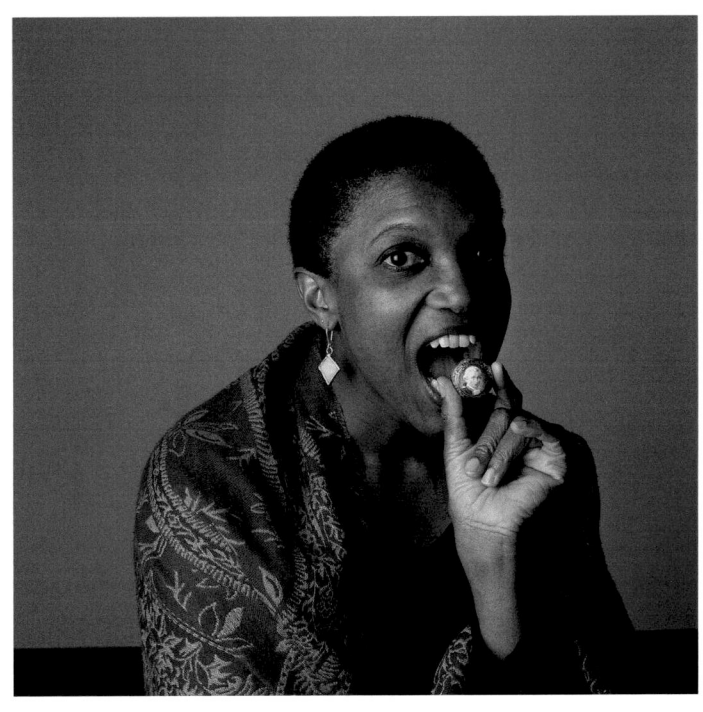

When I think about Mozart,
the words "profound simplicity" always come to mind.
To me, his music is so lyrical, his melodies so "vocal"
that they go straight to the heart in the most simple and direct way.
And for me, what touches my heart, touches my soul,
the vessel of my most profound emotions.

Claron McFadden

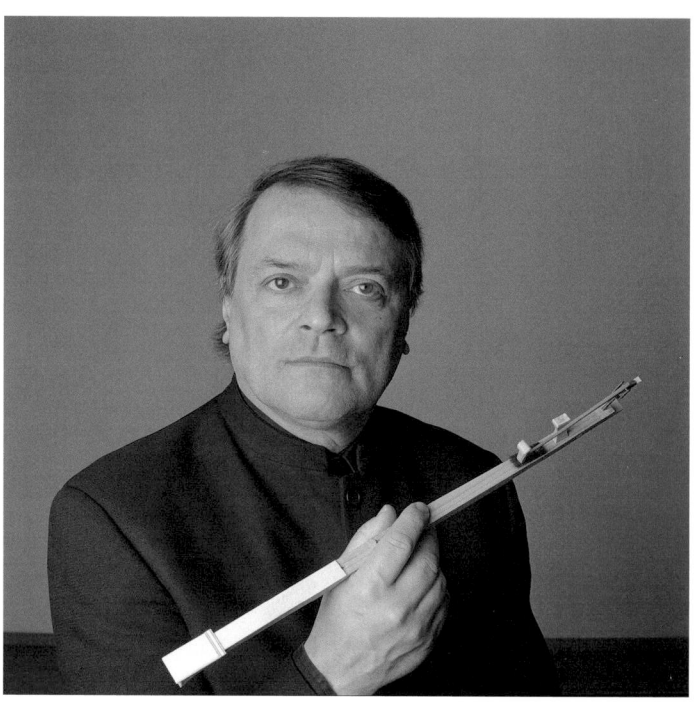

I regard Mozart's work as a perfect example of Art, as it was interpreted from the 16th till the 19th century: the perfect mastery of material. And this in all simplicity and honesty. No bombastic comments, no concealing facades, but an ever rich content, full of spirituality, inventiveness, humour and a feel for noble drama.

I wish the contemporary "wandering" artist to have all these qualities. We also learned from Mozart that trust is very important. In his handwritten documents, he only noted down what was strictly necessary and he put his trust in the musician during the performance, in his knowledge and skills and in the mastery of the obvious and good taste as well.

Indeed, without that trust there is no chance of success. I wish all those who today watch over 'the art' and pursue a policy to have this quality.

Jos van Immerseel

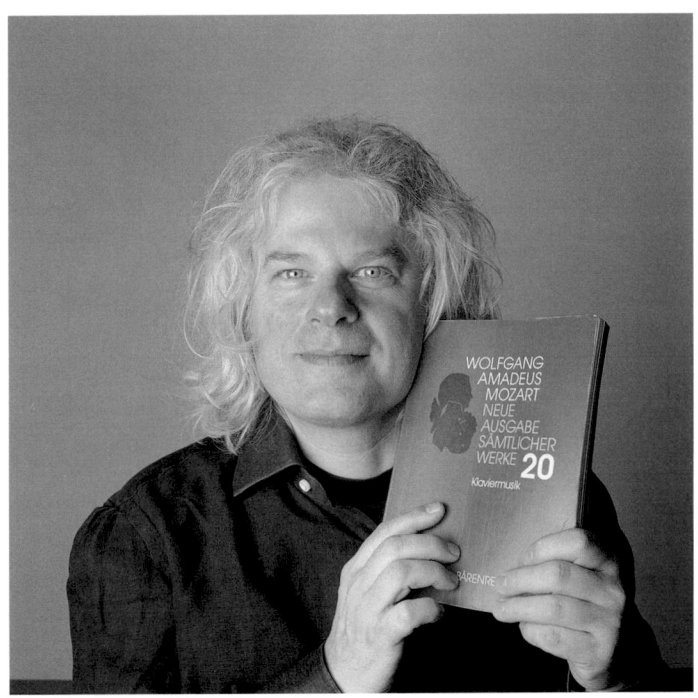

There comes a time in life when the pure taste of mineral water
becomes even dearer to you than the most sophisticated cocktail.

It is the same with Mozart:
with a minimum number of notes
he manages to spur a maximum emotion,
and it is this seemingly simplicity which turns
his music into something unique.

Ronald Brautigam

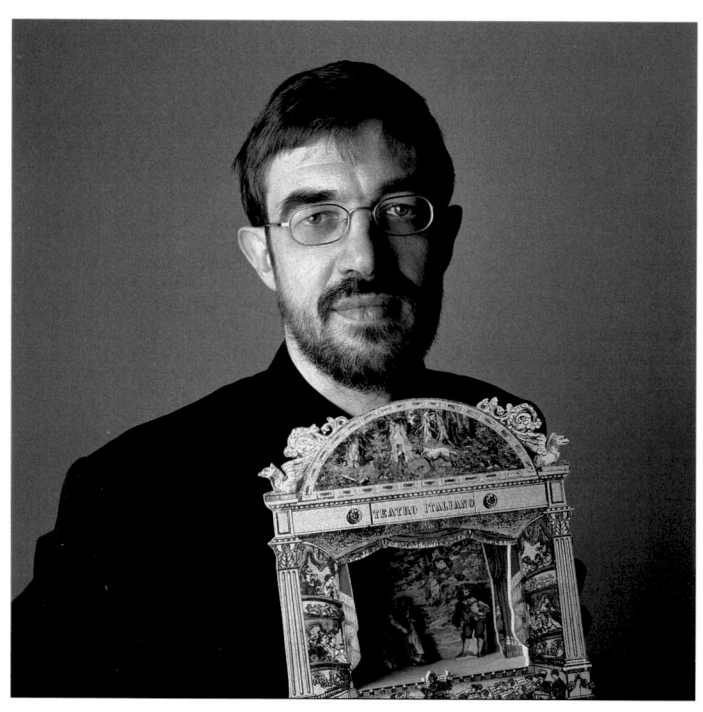

The essence of the genius of Wolfgang Amadeus Mozart can,
according to me, best be discovered through his operas:
a full range of human emotions, in a framework of ethereal
angels' chant and demonic subterranean forces.
– all this in the elusive costume of perfect, gracious beauty.

Jan Michiels

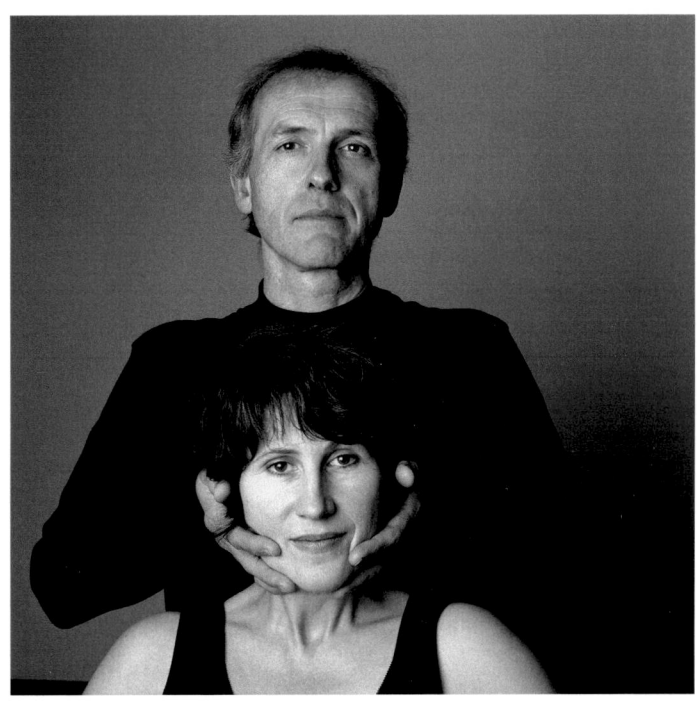

My relation to Mozart has been a rather limited one for a long time.
As a cellist – soloist – I never actively came into contact with his music.
I did play the Clarinet quintet about a hundred times in a chamber-music context...

Of course I was familiar with his string quartets, piano sonatas, concerti, symphonies etc. Brilliant, beautiful, grand. But not quite the love of my life. That love hit me when I discovered the string quintets. The directness, inventiveness, familiarity, liveliness and depth! I had only had such an all-embracing experience with Bach.

THE example to all composers that succeeded him. Superior in every way – harmony, counterpoint, structure, etc. – but mostly in the human aspect of the music. To use all those skills, all that talent, all that science with the intention to confront us with our humaneness. In these string quintets Mozart showed that he understood Bach's message. And therefore was able to transmit these wonderful emotions. This can only be done by someone who does not simply possess the genius but who, above all, has lived life and has truly loved.

Roel Dieltiens

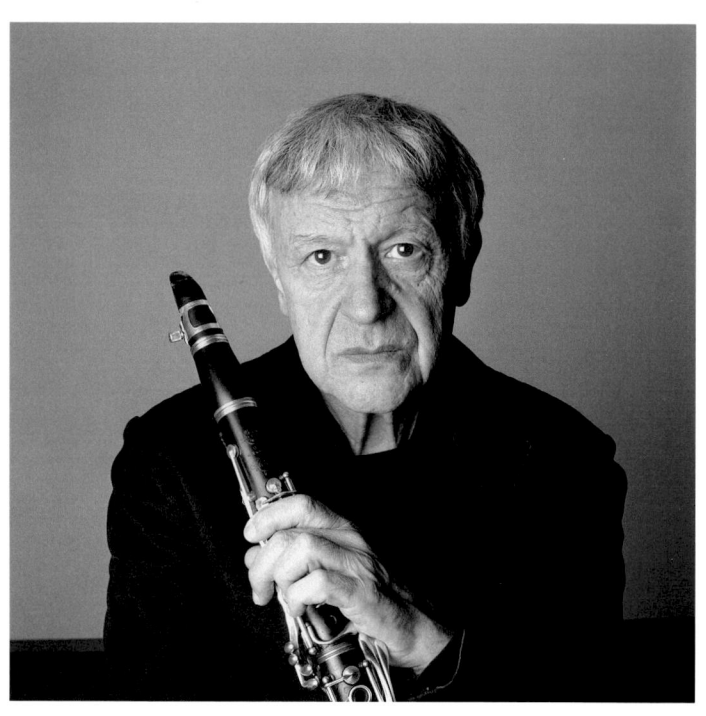

When you meet Mozart, you feel like a dancer on a rope.
His chant is so exceptional that while playing it,
you feel like you are being held by a rope
But your biggest fear is that it might slip away from you.

Michel Portal